COMFORTABLE COMPASSION?

COMFORTABLE COMPASSION?

Charles Elliott

HODDER AND STOUGHTON
LONDON SYDNEY AUCKLAND TORONTO

British Library Cataloguing in Publication Data

Elliott, Charles, *1939–*
   Comfortable compassion.
   1. Church and the poor
   I. Title
   261.8'3258   BV639.P6

   ISBN 0 340 40737 9

*Hodder and Stoughton Editorial Office: 47 Bedford Square, London
WC1B 3DP*

Dedication

This book was written while I was successively G. E. M. Scott Fellow at Ormond College, University of Melbourne, and Benjamin Meaker Professor at the University of Bristol. Its publication gives me the opportunity of thanking both universities for their welcome and generosity. I offer this book as a small token of my appreciation of their hospitality. While it is invidious to name individuals, I am particularly indebted, in various ways, to Rob Jackson, the Parkers, the Balabanskis, the Stents, the Beares and the Ekkels in Melbourne and to Michael Lee and Meg Davies and her lunch club in Bristol. And if that seems a long list for a slight volume, it shows how blessed I have been in my friends...

Acknowledgements

Professor Duncan Forrester of the University of Edinburgh, Dr Catherine Price of the University of Leicester and Stephen Cummins of the University of California were generous enough to read an early draft, and made many valuable suggestions for its improvement. Third year students in the Departments of Theology and Politics at the University of Bristol heard parts of the book as lectures and stimulated me to think out some of the issues more clearly. I am more than formally grateful to all of them.

Gwyneth Goodhead typed various drafts with her customary accuracy, speed and equanimity: I am very appreciative of all her help.

Chapter 1

1 Emergency

'One of the television channels is going to carry a film on the drought in Ethiopia. It will shock a lot of people, and so there may be some public response. The channel doesn't want to have to handle the cash. I'm calling a meeting of the Disasters Emergency Committee to consider it. Can you come?'

I swallowed hard. A hot July sun shimmered on the railway track outside my office window. High summer. Ethiopia. One film at a not very prime time. Hardly the stuff a huge appeal is made of. And we couldn't risk an appeal that went off at half-cock. The voluntary agencies need all the credibility they can muster. Some recent appeals had dented that credibility. A poor public response this time round could tear the Disasters Emergency Committee apart and lead us back to the bad old days of inter-agency rivalry and competition.

The meeting did little to allay any of these fears. The pre-viewed film was disappointing both technically and sub-stantially. My colleagues were all, as I was, half-hearted about an appeal, aware of the difficulty of stirring British interest in Ethiopia, a country with which we have historically had negligible contact.

After much low-key discussion, we decided to go ahead, bolstering each other's confidence that we might raise a million pounds or even one and a half million. We knew how wholly inadequate such a sum would be in the face of what we already realised would be a disaster of historic proportions; but we also knew, or thought we knew, that to expect to raise more would be a triumph of optimism over experience.

We were, as everyone now knows, spectacularly wrong. A fortnight later we had revised our expectations upwards – to two million pounds, to five million, to seven million. As the media story began to break world-wide, it became clear that the public response would be of a different order of magnitude to anything we had ever seen.

And as I write, sixteen months and Live Aid/Band Aid/Sport Aid later, that response shows little sign of abating. I have just been accosted on my way to my local supermarket and asked to buy something off the shelves and donate it on my way out – in this locality, a new phenomenon indeed.

The full story of this whole event has not yet been written. When it is, one of the most fascinating chapters will be on the public response in the UK, the United States, Europe and Australia. Just why *did* 'Ethiopia' become such a galvanising issue? Was it only a media event which became self-feeding after Geldof's intervention? That seems improbable, as there has been startling coverage of other famines and disasters, some of it attracting attention from entertainment stars (though arguably not pop-stars). Was it a metaphorical slap in the eye to the Marxist government? Doubtful if that explains much, since there is remarkably little sympathy for the poor in Marxist Cuba. Was it a final dawning of the obscenity (a word much used in this connection) of the contrast between the US and EEC wringing their hands over food surpluses, while the peasants of Ethiopia were wringing their hands in despair?

Maybe it was a combination of all of these factors and more besides. One thing is certain – the assumption that the relatively affluent peoples of the rich countries do not (and cannot be persuaded to) care about poor people in distant unknown lands is simply false. Despite scepticism about the effectiveness of emergency relief measures and cynicism about the good intentions of governments of whatever political colour (both well-founded in the Ethiopian case), here is nonetheless a humaneness, an empathy with the desperate that is seemingly almost universal. 'I'm no Good Samaritan,' I heard a City gent at the supermarket say, 'but there are some things you just can't ignore.' So said millions as they responded to Geldof's lead.

The difficulty is, of course, that for most of the time most of us are very adept at ignoring the iceberg of which the Ethiopian tragedy is only the tip. There is a curious, one might almost say pathological, discontinuity between an intense emotional commitment to a particularly dramatic symptom and a continuing neglect of the chronic disease of which that symptom is part.

There are good reasons for this pathology, not least an inability, or certainly an extreme reluctance, to expose ourselves to the psychic pain of empathy with the victims of that chronic disease. It is painful enough seeing one TV documentary on one village in the midst of one famine: I have seen tough men with tears streaming down their faces as they allow some of that pain in. To generalise from that one exposure to the hundreds of millions whose life chances are hardly better, and to go on doing that at real depth day after day, is to court a pain so acute, so overwhelming, that few could long survive it.

The pain is, of course, made more handleable by the prospect of relief. That is to say, we imagine, perhaps not wholly without foundation, that we can make a difference. Lives can be saved. Villages can be rebuilt. Children can be changed from gaunt spectres to normal healthy bouncing kids. Even though whatever we do will not be enough – so that some will die – at least there is a prospect of saving a few. Given that hope and the assurance that money given today will be translated into food the day after tomorrow, we can tolerate the pain of empathy because we can translate it into direct action that will have some beneficial effects.

2 Relief and Development

The contrast between emergency relief and long-term development lies in two dimensions. First, there is the contrast of scale. Horrifyingly large and extensive as it was, the African drought of 1983–85 was just that – it was a drought in Africa for a couple of years. No one is sure how many people were involved, but it would probably be of the order of ten million. Compare that with the 800 million who, on the World Bank's criteria, live in absolute poverty not for a year or two, and not just in a number of countries in one continent. They live in absolute poverty permanently in a very large number of countries on three continents. The 'Ethiopian crisis' was large but apprehensible – if only just. World poverty is barely within the grasp of the human mind.

Secondly the Ethiopian crisis, for all its logistical difficulties and confusions, seemed soluble in the sense that if enough food could be moved fast enough and far enough people could be prevented from dying. (That may be a very minimal sense of 'soluble', but it is not an unimportant one.) By contrast, overcoming the poverty of 800 million people on three continents does not seem a soluble problem in any equivalent sense. 'It just makes me despair,' said a recent graduate. She was speaking for us all. When we contemplate the larger picture, we are not contemplating a problem that can be solved by any quantity of money or logistics or self-sacrifice or effort by well-intentioned volunteers. We are moving into a totally different order of being. Despair seems the only honest response.

If these are some of the basic human drives that lead us to pay greater attention to disasters than to chronic poverty, they are reinforced, at least on the face of it, by much Christian preaching. A paradigm case is that of the Good Samaritan. As usually interpreted, the parable suggests that Jesus was encouraging his disciples to meet acute human need wherever they saw it. Reinforced by both Pauline and Pastoral epistles, Jesus' teachings seem to put a high premium on selfless caring for the afflicted. 'In so far as you have done it to the least of these my brothers, you have done it to me.' The emphasis is on immediate action – on feeding the hungry, on clothing the naked, healing the sick, visiting the imprisoned, bringing comfort to the afflicted. Standing in the tradition of Elijah and Elisha, Jesus is presented in the synoptic Gospels as one who acts to relieve immediate suffering.

Parallel to that whole train of thought goes a tradition that pre-dates the eighth century prophets and which reaches its most vigorous expression in the epistle of St James, incorporating a hostile attitude to wealth. To hang on to wealth when others are in need receives continuous condemnation from over a thousand years of biblical writing. That tradition is maintained not only by the early Church fathers, but by a whole series of rediscoveries of radical discipleship, from the Hussites and the Levellers, to John and Charles Wesley and the Christian Socialists and their disparate successors today.

Put together the biblical command to relieve immediate need and the no less biblical antagonism to wealth in the face of immediate need, and it is little wonder that there is a long Christian tradition of responding to disasters and emergencies.

To this extent, the response to the Ethiopian crisis, from the early reluctant stages that I have described to the showbiz euphoria of Band Aid and its equivalents, stands squarely in a long tradition. It is not part of the argument of this book to belittle or in any way detract from that tradition. It is important to emphasise that right at the start. It is sometimes assumed that those of us who think that it is now time to move on from this level of response are unsympathetic to or dismissive of this whole tradition of immediate relief. 'How many hospitals or hospices do you see founded by or built to honour Marxists?' I was once asked. The implication is that Marxists, or those who might vulgarly be assumed to think like them, are so busy changing the system that they have no time for the system's victims. I cannot speak for Marxists: they are more than competent to speak for themselves. For my own part, I want to start by repeating with all the emphasis at my command that I am proud of the Christian tradition of immediate relief; of emergency aid, of spontaneous acts of love towards whoever needs them. Furthermore, I do not regard a continuation of such work as in any way inconsistent with or superseded by the approaches I shall be outlining in the rest of this book.

3 A Look Ahead

I shall, however, want to argue that Christian thinking about poverty, injustice and oppression has not been very successful in the realm of either action or ideas when it comes to moving beyond immediate caring. If that seems an exaggeration, let me quote one revealing statistic. In 1983 all the British overseas development charities – from the relatively large ones like Oxfam and Save the Children to the many tiddlers supporting one hospital in India or one school book programme in Tanzania – together raised around fifty million pounds from the British public. That money was spent on the short- and long-term relief of the poverty of 800 million people. The Ethiopian appeal, affecting approximately ten million people, raised exactly the same sum of money in one year. The conclusion seems inescapable; the call for immediate relief in the face of famine and large-scale loss of life mobilises us in a way that enabling people to break out of degrading poverty does not.

The paradox is that everyone knows that immediate relief is only that – immediate relief. The Chinese proverb – give a man a fish and you feed him for a day; teach a man to fish and you feed him for a lifetime – is a cliché that is trotted out in every forum where these matters are discussed. The truth behind that cliché has not, of course, been despised by the Churches. Indeed, it triggered the explosive growth in Church-related development agencies from the late fifties to the present day. Nonetheless the figures speak for themselves. We Christians are more easily persuaded that the Gospel demands action in an emergency than we are that it demands a constant commitment to the poor and the oppressed.

In that, of course, we are not much different from the governments of the rich world. The response of those governments to the facts of world poverty has always been inadequate and, since the oil price revolution and the rise of the New Right, it has become steadily less adequate. This hardening of policy is not only a matter of declining quality and/or quantity of aid: more crucially there has also been a deterioration in the trade, technology and investment milieux in which the poor countries have to operate.

We shall have more to say about this later. For the moment, I want merely to introduce an idea that will recur throughout this book. I shall be arguing that, in responding to mass poverty in an age of plenty, the Churches have become stuck with a specific concept of the problem and of their role in response to that problem. I want to show that their concept of the problem is not false but inadequate and largely self-defeating; and that it has led the Churches into a cul-de-sac of well-intentioned but largely ineffective gestures, while leaving the real issues either unidentified or neglected.

Some readers will groan at this point and assume that I shall be making the case for more radical action by the big Church development agencies – World Vision, Tear Fund, Christian Aid, Church World Service or their many counterparts in the rich countries. I do not deny that much of my argument has that implication. The main point however, is that the Church – that is Christians like you and me – has too easily sloughed off the problem on to the development agencies. 'We have set up specialist organisations to meet that need – and now we can leave it to them.' No. The issues we are facing, I shall argue, are not *of that kind*. World poverty is not like an earthquake in Mexico City or a landslide in Hong Kong – or, for that matter, a drought in Africa. It is not, that is to say, a one-off (or even three-off) tragic incident which can be 'put right' by the intervention of the specialists.

The poverty of 800 million, rising to one billion by the end of the century is, I shall argue, *the outcome of a process*. That process is not random or unintended: it is the direct result of mechanisms that enrich some as surely as they impoverish others. As such, it is the outworking of the power of some over others, and it is the nature of that relationship – of the powerful over the powerless – that it distributes wealth to the former at the expense of the latter.

The use of power, I shall argue in the last chapters, is essentially – i.e. in its essence – a religious question. Of course it also has economic, social and legal aspects, but exploitation of the weak by the strong is an issue so fundamental to human well-being that it is a recurrent theme in the biblical record of God's love for his people. In addition, we must remember that the early Church interpreted the life, death and resurrection of Jesus Christ in terms of power.

We are not then, dealing with narrow technical issues about the criteria Church agencies should use in selecting projects for their funding; nor even the more interesting questions about the nature of the relationship between a rich North Atlantic donor agency and a struggling co-operative in rural Africa. Certainly, we shall need to look at both those questions – and many more beside. The central argument of the book, however, is that these are second or third order questions, by comparison with the first order question about the ways in which the powerful deal with the powerless – and vice versa. I shall insist that this question is a religious one – and as such asks us to look again at the nature of our obedience to our Lord and saviour.

The organisation of the text is, I hope, fairly straight-forward. Because some of the material might be unfamiliar to the reader, I have adopted a more or less historical approach in order to give the exposition a skeleton. Beginning with the

colonial period in Africa and Asia, I take a very brief look at
the role the Churches played in development – and, more
importantly, how they conceived of development. Then I
consider the changes that occurred as a result of political
independence in Asia and Africa and the contemporaneous
burst of interest in development in the international community, the ecumenical community and individual Christians.
We shall see how that has shaped the structure of the Churches'
response to world poverty both in the rich North and the poor
South. We shall, however, have to review the ways in which
understandings of the nature of world poverty have changed
since the mid-1960s, and the response such new insights have
evoked from the Churches. We shall find that most of these
new approaches focus on power as a key explanatory variable,
and that will lead us, in the last chapters, to think about a
theology and spirituality of power.

I have tried to avoid being heavy and over-abstract in the
hope that the many people who wonder what is, could be and
should be an adequate response to world poverty, will find
something in these pages that they can use for further
reflection. Inevitably, I have had to sacrifice rigour and
comprehensiveness in the interest of intelligibility. For those
who want to study some of the issues at a greater depth than I
have attempted here, I have tried to indicate some of the key
works in the endnotes. It would be misleading, however, to
pretend that this is a simple detached account. That it is not. I
believe that the Churches have become trapped in a set of
attitudes and institutions that sell short both the Christian
Gospel and the poor of the world. To that extent this book is a
plea – a plea for a fresh look, a radical reinterpretation, a new
start.

Chapter 2

1 Mission and Development

The Churches have been involved in development since the early days of missionary activity in what was then the Empire – whether British, French or Portuguese. Schools, hospitals and farms – even experimental plant-breeding establishments – were the common coinage of missionary activity, particularly in Africa where white settlement (in the so-called settler colonies of east and central Africa) offered both particular challenges and particular opportunities. It is not part of my purpose to assess the impact, for good and ill, of those early missionary activities.[1]

For during the 1950s a marked division occurred between the mission activities of the Church and its nascent 'development' activities. We shall review some of the reasons for this bifurcation later on in this chapter: our immediate task is to explain the nature of this division. What was seen as 'mission'; what as 'development'?

It is hardly an oversimplification to say that in the 1950s and 1960s mission in the developing world (still, of course, comprised mostly of colonies in Africa and Asia, in contrast to Latin America) was defined as what missionaries did. And what missionaries did varied immensely from one denominational tradition to another, from one country to another; from one 'sending agency' to another. For mission strategy was constantly under debate: how did one prepare 'primitive' people to receive the Word of God? how was that Word best proclaimed? what elements of local culture could justifiably be incorporated in the life of the Church and what had to be withstood (or eliminated altogether with the help of the secular authorities)?

Answers to such basic questions naturally varied. Nonetheless the notion of pre-mission, of preparing the people, was almost universally espoused – except for a number of extreme evangelical groups, mostly from the United States, who had little sympathy with what they saw as diversions from the main work of proclamation. This work of pre-mission had two basic thrusts, each capable of much elaboration.

First came the task of raising the intellectual understanding of the people so that they could for example, read the scriptures or the hymnal and develop a set of concepts that could contain the key elements of Christian revelation. (That their own language and religious consciousness often had closely analogous concepts was sometimes – and increasingly – recognised.) This task, it was assumed, meant a major commitment to education for, in many Victorian minds, literacy and religion were regarded as inseparable.

It is no surprise to find, then, that by the end of the colonial period, the missions, taken together, were the major providers of education in most African countries, and very substantial providers even in the Indian sub-continent where missionary penetration had been much less complete. Even there, it is significant to note, the high quality schools from which would be drawn the first élites of the post-independence period were, without exception, mission-related.

This arrangement suited the colonial powers well enough. True, there were sometimes sharp disputes between the settlers, who wanted a pliant but technically equipped workforce, and the missionaries who, in general, had a less functional view of education. Such disputes posed problems for the colonial administration, but since it funded a proportion of the missions' educational work, it had relatively little difficulty in holding the ring. A threat to reduce the level of funding was usually enough to bring a fractious mission into line.

The second thrust of pre-mission work might be called love in practice. Christianity had to be shown to be about love of neighbour. Indeed, many missionaries expected their works to communicate the real nature of the Gospel more effectively than their preaching or teaching. Caritative activities of all kinds were therefore part of the mainstream work of the missions – from orphanages to hospitals; from asylums to girls' hostels; from workshops for the blind to homes of rest for the elderly.

Again, there was a neat division of labour with the colonial administration. Although in general official funding of these activities was less generous than in the case of education, it suited the colonial powers to leave 'welfare work' to the missionaries and anyone else who would organise it. Such work took some of the sting out of colonialism and thereby helped to legitimate the régime – an increasingly significant contribution as nationalist consciousness developed after the Second World War.

Taken together, however, these two thrusts are unlikely to remain static, for each has its own dynamic, and to a degree those dynamics work together. For example, even basic education is likely to raise demands for a better life-style, not only in economic terms, but in political and social terms too. Educated young men (the education of girls lagged woefully, even into the 1970s) were not content to return to their shambas and submit to the unsympathetic discipline of their elders. They wanted a job; a future; relief from the tedium of village life. Many migrated to town in search of those benefits, and those better qualified to cope with urban life secured them. The more far-sighted and less conservative missionaries began to try to equip their protegés with the qualifications that would enable them to cope – artisan skills; technical diplomas; teaching certificates, or even, for a tiny minority, degrees.

As an educated élite emerged, faster in West Africa than in settler-dominated East Africa, so questions of participation in political power became more urgent. Less obviously, the same questions were being generated by the internal dynamics of the Church's caritative work. Missions were, for example, amongst the harshest critics of the migratory labour system developed by the mining companies of Central and South Africa, for they came into contact with the pastoral and community effects of that system. In the same way, missionaries in the rural areas of settler colonies saw the effects of the alienation of land to settlers and the forced settlement of peasants in Nature Reserves.

Certainly the protests of the missionaries were muted, and always originated from a small minority. For protest was not welcomed by the colonial administration – nor, it has to be said, by any Church leaders in the colonies and in the metropolitan power. In their view it was much preferable to work *with* the secular powers rather than against them: and there was plenty of opportunity to do so in the name of improving the condition of the people.

Perhaps a hangover from Victorian England; perhaps a half-conscious attempt to reconcile the inner contradictions of colonialism; probably a largely intuitive response to the juxtaposition of need and opportunity, many missionaries found themselves heavily involved in what one tradition called 'village improvement'. Sometimes this meant no more than commending a village headman for a well-kept village and promising a small reward if he could persuade his neighbouring headman to follow his example. Occasionally it meant much more than that, not only at the micro, village level, but also at the national and even international level. The introduction of cotton-growing into Uganda and its rapid extension through the missionary controlled Uganda Company not only made viable the railway from Kampala to the coast – an important economic and strategic objective of the Colonial Office in London – but also secured for Lancashire a supply of cotton at a favourable price when the industry was facing fierce competition from American textile interests.[2]

Another example can be taken from West Africa. There is little doubt that the Basle Mission played a key, if unplanned, role in the introduction of cocoa-farming to what was then the Gold Coast. The Mission played a less entrepreneurial role than the Uganda Company, but both by supplying technical support and, more extensively, by the provision of training and the demonstration that technical change could be profitable, the Mission played a fulcral role in a development that changed the course of economic and political history in West Africa.[3]

It is important to get the nuance right at this point. It is not part of my argument that the missions were universally and constantly ahead of their times in championing the cause of the oppressed and deprived. Nor do I seek to deny the close identity of interest between the colonial administration and many of the missions – an identity that opens the Church to the charge of allowing itself to be co-opted by the secular powers. Nor do I deny that racism and attitudes of ethnic superiority sometimes informed the policies and life-styles of the missions. No, we have to see the great missionary expansion of 1880–1914 in its historical context and recognise that many of the structures and attitudes changed slowly over the next forty years. In no sense, then, do I wish to whitewash the record of the missions in Africa and Asia. I do, however, want to lay emphasis on the historical background of the Church's involvement in what today would be called development, because we can only understand what has happened since 1960 by being aware of this background.

For, as I have already indicated, the Church in the metropolitan countries – and, to an extent, in the developing world – almost forgot this background when 'development' became an imperative for the Churches after 1960. Before we analyse this odd turn of events, it will be helpful to consider what the Churches understood by 'development' as it emerged as a major priority in the 1960s. We shall have much more to say about this in the next chapter. Suffice it to mention at this point that the Churches, perhaps inevitably, acquired from contemporary discussion a notion of development that was heavily economistic, materialistic, technocratic and centralistic. Development was all but identified with economic growth, and the assumption was that economic growth could be secured by governmental manipulation of a few economic variables, such as savings, investment, and exports.

2 Mission and Development Separated

The 'universe of disclosure' of economists and planners, central to secular understandings of development in the early 1960s, seemed far removed from the work and experience of missionaries. There was a culture gap, a language gap between the two worlds. That, however, does not adequately explain the course of events – events that drive a structural and theological wedge between mission and development which has impoverished the latter even more than the former. Where do we have to look for a more adequate explanation?

First, the great spurt in development activity coincided with the granting of political independence to former colonies.[4] That event caught the missionary societies, if not on the wrong foot, then unsure of their sense of direction. While the leaders of many newly independent countries paid lavish tribute to the work of the missionaries, that praise was tinged with challenge.[5] For most Churches in most countries had been dominated by expatriate missionaries. Indeed, in some African Churches, the number of black ministers or priests at the time of independence could literally be counted on the fingers of one hand. The Church was thus an ecclesiastical reflection of a political reality. The whites held power. When the political reality changed, the new African leadership looked for equivalent changes in the Churches.

That was not all. As we have seen, in Africa and the Caribbean, and to a lesser extent in India and Sri Lanka, the Churches controlled a large segment of what we would normally regard as the public service – schools, hospitals, teacher training colleges, even universities. Pledged to expand and improve these public services, newly independent governments sought to wrest control of them from the Church: and that usually meant from expatriate missionary societies.

This posed a fundamental challenge to the whole strategy of Roman Catholic and many Protestant mission agencies, who had come to see the provision of these services as an essential part of pre-mission, a point of entry into the communities they were seeking to evangelise.[6] It may be over-crude to represent education and health care as a lure to attract converts (since there is much evidence of the provision of such services without any attempt to proselytise either directly or indirectly). Nonetheless, the prospect of divesting themselves of a large part of their assets – and the activities associated with those assets – threw the missionary societies into a period of considerable turmoil as they reassessed their whole strategy.

Third, the forces that led newly independent governments to challenge the mission societies with respect both to national leadership of the Church and control of public services, also made them suspicious of missionary involvement in development projects. Certainly there are many exceptions. Some leaders, most notably Julius Nyerere of Tanzania and Kenneth Kaunda of Zambia, were sufficiently perceptive to see that a blanket refusal to co-operate with missionaries in new styles of work was as unjust as it was unwise. Nonetheless, the full force of nationalism combined with a popular perception of the missionaries as agents of the colonial power to make unwelcome, at less exalted levels of government, co-operation between state and mission in the new flush of development activity that accompanied independence.

Fourth, many of the new leaders at both national and local level were, as is often stressed, products of missionary schools: some, however, were also people who had fallen foul of the missionary apparatus. In Kenya, for instance, even as early as the 1930s, the leaders of the nationalist movement had been educated in mission schools: but they had been victims of racially discriminatory policies when they sought either to extend their education or to gain employment in mission-based institutions.[7] It was simply unrealistic to expect people whose political consciousness had been formed in reaction against a racist missionary background to co-operate in the euphoric days of independence with the very people they identified as part of the problem.

Fifth, in the metropolitan countries, political independence of the former colonies brought with it a reluctance to give priority to the whole missionary endeavour. Many factors were at work here. These ranged from post-imperial weariness and an erosion of self-confidence, to a greater or lesser degree of willingness to stand back from direct involvement while independence took root. At its best, this was a deliberate choice to give the newly independent countries 'space' to find their own way.

Other more human factors played a role too. Paternalistic attitudes towards 'our black brothers' began to look absurd as these black brothers regularly berated the British at the UN and at Commonwealth meetings. It became increasingly hard to recruit clergy, and particularly lay people, to work in countries that could offer no security and in Churches that could offer no careers.

3 The Ecumenical Imperative

For these reasons, then, the development activities of the Churches tended to be conceived and organised separately from, and in many cases, in opposition to, the traditional missionary structures of the Church. There was, however, a further dimension. At least as far as the Protestant Churches were concerned the main thrust – intellectual, political, even ecclesiological – for the Church's involvement in development came through the ecumenical movement. The role of the World Council of Churches' Uppsala Assembly was formative rather than critical, but it gave both a higher visibility and a more incisive rationale for the involvement of the ecumenical community in the liberation of peoples from hunger, disease and superstition. The bad old days of denominational rivalry which had led to the duplication of schools and hospitals (and therefore to the inefficient use of resources) were contrasted with the opportunity to express the growing unity of the Church in the hard physical fact of common work to raise living standards of under-privileged people.

Thus Eugene Carson Blake, the American General Secretary of the World Council of Churches, told an international ecumenical consultation on development in 1970:

> If we as Churches have any particular claim to make, it is that we are a world-wide community crossing national and racial barriers. Our involvement in development should enable us to manifest this characteristic of the church ... The vision that beckons the Churches to move forward in the concern for development is the vision of the one human family ... [8]

This aspiration chimed well with the rhetoric of the new leadership in the developing world. In many British colonies, for example, sectarian strife had been so bitter that it had become necessary physically to divide the country between the various denominations. Thus one tribal group would be Roman Catholic, another tribal group would be Presbyterian, a third would be Anglican. The new political leaders were faced with the problem of producing a level of national consciousness that transcended traditional tribal barriers – and denominational rivalries. From the standpoint of African or Caribbean political leaders, then, if the Churches were going to be involved in development, it was far preferable that they be involved ecumenically rather than denominationally. Yet this was a demand that, almost by definition, was beyond the capacity of the missionary societies to meet.

I emphasise the historical roots of the distinction between development and mission for a particular purpose which will become apparent as the argument unfolds. Suffice it for now to say that the historical forces that detached development activity from missionary activity and, more important, the missionary experience and thinking of the Churches, left the development activities exposed. They were exposed in two senses. They were exposed first and perhaps most fatally to the *Zeitgeist*, the prevailing ideology, of the secular development debate. And second, they were exposed to their own internal dynamics without the corrective of a theological critique which was available but unheard (and/or misunderstood) in the longer missionary tradition of the Church.

4 The Secular Setting

Only rarely do understandings of the Church's vocation develop quite independently of changes in secular thought. In most cases, religious conviction adds a moral imperative and a particular language to a secular movement that originates in the interplay of deep social forces. The abolition of slavery on both sides of the Atlantic is one example. The campaign for factory legislation is another. We shall not be surprised to find, therefore, that the Church's involvement in development followed – both chronologically and in many respects ideologically – fashions dictated by the secular world.

This is not to criticise or belittle what was done, nor the process by which considerable progress was achieved. There was a kind of historical inevitability about these processes. This was new territory, a new challenge. Sensing the need to produce results (though never precisely what was to be the nature of those results) the Churches had to pick up ideas, people, plans, programmes from wherever they could. Indeed, the thinking had to run to keep up with the action. The large German Catholic development agency, Misereor, for instance, started work with no substantive theories about the nature of development or the ambiguity of Western interventions in developing societies. Large sums of money were becoming available and the emphasis was on action. The voices of caution, of doubt about both the wisdom of so easy an accommodation to this fashion and about the competence of the Churches to fulfil the promises they were making, were drowned out in the rush to show that in a post-imperialist age, the Churches had a valid role in the developing world.

In the next chapter we need to look at this issue more deeply. What was the nature of the ideology that the Churches were absorbing, often only half-consciously, from the secular environment? How did that ideology combine with other pressures to push the Churches' witness in a particular direction? What form, what physical form, did that witness take? These are the questions we shall be addressing.

We shall set the argument in a lightly-sketched historical perspective, to continue to emphasise the role of history in shaping the life of the Church, and to deliver us from the slick judgments of hindsight. It is well to remember, however, that like a bad smell, history tends to linger. The styles of thought and action we shall be examining are historically generated – but existentially enduring. They may have been superseded at some level of the Church's life. Ideas, however, are rather like technology. The new takes longer to drive out the old than we often recognise. The historical dimension of the next chapters, then, is important: but it should not mislead us into thinking we have transcended our own history.

Chapter 3

1 The Secular Margins of Development Policy

In the last chapter we looked at some of the background to the Church's involvement in development, and we noticed that the involvement drew heavily from the secular debates of the time. To take that further, we need to sketch in some of the forces that lay behind attempts by Western governments to fashion both a rationale and a strategy in their dealings with the newly independent countries of the Third World.

In the wake of the Korean War, the domino theory held an unassailably dominant position in geopolitical and strategic thinking in the United States and Europe alike. As the tide of independence – or to quote a better known meteorological analogy, the wind of change – had strengthened, so the fear grew that one country 'going communist' in the developing world would inevitably lead to a vast expansion of Soviet domination. The Suez Canal, the Middle Eastern oilfields, the Cape route, and the network of British, French and American bases in the Indian Ocean and the Pacific were thought to be a risk. Containing the 'communist threat' required, from the West, a broad mix of policies. A vastly increased development aid programme was valued as an essential ingredient in that mix. Under its voluminous skirts could be secured political, strategic, military and commercial policies which, taken together, would make it extremely costly for a newly independent country in the developing world to throw in its lot with the Soviet bloc.

Commercial considerations probably played a much smaller general role, though in particular cases access to raw materials, e.g. tin and rubber in Malaysia, loomed large. In Europe more than in the United States, naive post-war expectations of the great economic advantage to be gained from the developing world had largely evaporated, though some companies, particularly mining companies – Amex, Rio Tinto Zinc, Road Selection Trust – had, in the late fifties and much of the sixties extremely profitable investments to defend. Such companies were not without political influence. This was even more true of some of the very large US companies with profitable operations in Latin America, the Caribbean (especially Cuba) and the Philippines: their influence was later, as in Chile, shown to be decisive.

A third rationale had less to do with geopolitics and economic strategy than with diplomacy and international public relations. The vast majority of newly independent states became members of the United Nations and its increasingly significant specialised agencies such as the World Heath Organisation, the International Labour Office, and UNESCO. Many of them also became full members of the various institutions of the international monetary system, most notably the International Monetary Fund, but there their influence could be minimised since the metropolitan powers had ensued that voting was weighted by wealth. Nonetheless, even in those institutions, but more so in the General Assembly of the United Nations, significant aggregations of developing countries clustering around one of the giants like India or Brazil could, at the very least, make things diplomatically awkward for the Western powers. Aid could be used both as carrot and stick. There is plenty of evidence that it was so used, particularly to secure favourable votes in the General Assembly at times of international tension.[1]

None of this is to deny there was also a genuine humanitarian concern. There clearly was, particularly among some of the major professional figures such as Paul Hoffman and Dag Hammerskjöld, who played a leading role in shaping international co-operation for development. Humanitarian concern does not, however cut much ice with hard-nosed legislators. 'There are no votes in development', is a cliché I have heard again and again in the House of Commons. Congressmen would have said the same, but with greater emphasis. For them the only way to extract large sums of money from a reluctant Congress was to emphasise, and if necessary exaggerate, the geopolitical argument. That inevitably had baleful consequences, to which we shall have to return.

2 The Churches Respond

The Churches were not, of course, unaware of these considerations. For the fundamentalist right, both Roman Catholic and Protestant, the 'Keep Communists Out' argument justified, indeed demanded, the thorough-going involvement of the Churches. Mainstream, Liberal/ecumenical thinking, however, followed more closely the secular humanitarian view that colonialism had largely failed to raise living standards to a level consistent with human dignity and that it was now, in a period of unprecedented economic expansion in Europe and America, a moral duty to make good the deficiencies of the colonial period – and make them good fast.

It would be easy to demonstrate that much – from the French Jesuit Noel Drogart's careful and early demonstration of the relative deprivation of the developing world,[2] to Blake's round condemnation of that deprivation as 'moral outrage' twelve years later. We need however to tread cautiously. For there was (and in many ways still is) a long spectrum of Church opinion, even 'official' Church opinion. Indeed there is not just one spectrum; rather there is a family of spectra. For example, there is a range of opinion that stretches from the cautious operational agencies whose major focus is still in works of a caritative nature, to the analytical, social science trained Christian who takes a much more 'progressive' view of the nature of poverty and the Church's role in eradicating it. Then there is a range of opinion defined by theological or ecclesiastical background – from the Vatican to the Bible-belt of the United States. There is yet another range of opinion defined by country of origin: the voices of Central America are likely to be very different to the voices of India or Indonesia.

This is no academic point for it has two important corollaries. The first is that we are likely to find a large discontinuity between, let us say, the major papers at a World Council of Churches conference on the one hand, and the working hypothesis of a Church development agency in the US or the UK or Germany on the other. Despite the discontinuity, the two sets of ideas will interact, (or, at least, that is the hope of the WCC) the one influencing the other. Nonetheless, it is misleading to assume that the one gives us much insight into the other. Put concretely, we should not regard WCC statements (and a *fortiori* consultation papers) as descriptive of how Church development activists thought – or think.

The second corollary is that groups of the like-minded nucleate round particular issues, cutting across established lines of division. For example, on questions of development policy one may well find Brazilian Dominicans, Salvadorean Jesuits, South African charismatics and European liberal-evangelicals thinking on the same lines. A less fictional example is that of the Sojourners community in the United States. Originally evangelical in origin and inspiration, it now has a fifty per cent Catholic membership, and has taken a leading and highly visible role on issues of peace and justice.

With these two points in mind, it comes as no surprise to find formal declarations and publications from the Church – both Protestant and Catholic – using a different language and addressing a different problem to that of the Church development agencies on the ground. To put it crudely, a gap exists between the rhetoric of the Church's *thinking* bodies and the actions of the Church's acting bodies. Let us take one example. As early as 1963, the World Council of Churches was commissioning documents that spelt out, in uncompromising terms, a view of development that put the distribution and use of power at the centre of the process.

Summarising three papers from leading Churchmen from Africa and Asia, Paul Abrecht, a figure of considerable influence in progressive Protestant circles, wrote:

The question of world economic justice... arises in the relations between the rich and poor countries because there is no structure of world economic order... The present structures perpetuate the power of the richer ones and their ability to shape world economic development in a manner that suits primarily their own interests, their own philosophy of economic welfare and their conception of world economic progress. The essays... point to the sense of injustice which this monopoly of power arouses in the peoples of the poor nations.[3]

It is no exaggeration to say that, in progressive ecumenical circles, the following ten years saw a gradual elaboration of that position. We shall therefore need to return to it in a later chapter. For the moment, however, we have to recognise the difference in tone, timbre and content between an analysis of poverty couched essentially in terms of power, and the analysis with which, often only half consciously, the church agencies were operating. It is to a consideration of the latter to which we must now return.

3 The Church development agencies: ideas

Drawing heavily on rather unrefined understandings of the economic history of the developed world and, interestingly, on the particular economic features of Israel (for it was the Israeli economy that produced some of the influential early work on development), secular views of development gave pride of place to raising the level of per capita income, i.e. to economic growth. Indeed, growth and development were terms that were often used interchangeably: when they were differentiated, development was frequently understood as economic growth plus some improvement in social conditions, e.g. education, health, housing and employment.

The argument was beguilingly simple. Improving living conditions requires higher income. Higher incomes can only be achieved by improved productivity. Greater productivity requires higher investment. It is the task of international co-operation to provide a proportion of that development and thereby start the engine of growth (in a phrase that quickly became a cliché). It was recognised early on that the 'engine of growth' would bring about social change – urbanisation, a new class structure, a new range of tastes and expectations. These, however, were to be welcomed – welcomed in the name of modernisation.

For the key concept that came to describe the development effort of the 1950s and 1960s was that of modernisation. Given intellectual weight by Gunnar Mydral in his influential book *Asian Drama*,[4] the essence of modernisation theory was that the institutions – and behind the institutions, the thought-patterns of people in the developing countries – were unsuitable for economic growth towards a highly industrialised society. Institutions, perceptions, attitudes, ways of relating to each other therefore needed 'modernisation'. If these societies could be modernised (which usually was taken to mean become pale reflections of America), then they could achieve high economic growth rates, and ultimately the levels of consumption of America and Northern Europe.

The Church's thinking, particularly in the 'development agencies', was deeply penetrated by the ideology of modernisation. Indeed, it would have been more than surprising if the Churches had been able to resist so powerful and so universally acclaimed an ideology.

Take one revealing example. In an essay in one of the widely-quoted preparatory volumes to the 1966 Conference on Church and Society of the World Council of Churches, *Economic growth in World Perspective*, a Nigerian professor has this to say:

> It is only where the people are prepared for growth that all the other factors of growth –labour, capital and entrepreneurship – can become effective tools. The first prerequisite for growth, therefore, is for a nation to discover itself, to alert its people, to remove most of the social, political or economic handicaps and be determined to push ahead. An economy dominated by tradition-bound citizens, manorial lords and the belief in witchcraft and mystiques (sic) is not ready for growth...[5]

It is no surprise to discover that the author had written his doctorate at the University of London, had published a book on *Christianity and Communism* and was a leading layman in the Methodist Church in Nigeria. Virtually a symbol of modernisation himself, his views, as a technically qualified black layman, were inevitably (and in some ways not improperly) given great weight at a time when the ecumenical community was trying to come to terms with the poverty/development issue.

4 The Church development agencies: action

In terms of the Church's active involvement, one can detect a marked shift from the mid-1960s onwards from the traditional caritative activities of providing schools and hospitals and orphanages and old people's homes (areas in which the mission societies, incidentally, remained heavily involved for at least another fifteen years) to projects that reflected perfectly the modernisation paradigm. Vocational schools were established to produce 'modern' apprentices and partisans. Model farms were established to produce 'modern' agricultural techniques and to 'modernise' the farming systems of the peasants. Wells were dug, irrigation channels constructed, new breeds of cattle introduced to 'modernise' the whole agricultural sector. 'Modern' forms of economic organisation, like cooperatives and credit unions, were introduced to bring incentives and discipline to the assumedly lazy and backward peasantries.

For that is the inevitable implication of modernisation theory – namely that what exists is backward, inferior, opposed to and in conflict with progress, and generally lacking all those positive attributes that have enabled the Western industrial countries to 'succeed'. The implicit racism of this view hardly needs highlighting, but the ignorance behind it does. It ignores for example, the subtlety of social organisation in an Indian village or an African tribe. It ignores the astonishing technical knowledge of many indigenous people of their environment and its constraints. It ignores the delicacy of personal relationships and the wisdom of rural people in every continent. To deflect the charge of romanticism, let me give one or two examples.

For many years eager agricultural officers of colonial régimes implored and bullied peasants into growing pure stands of one particular crop, be it maize or beans or millet. It is only very recently that agricultural scientists have realised the great benefits to be gained from inter-cropping – mutual protection from pests and diseases, mutual shading, the fixation of nitrogen by the legumes in forms that can be immediately appropriated by the cereals. Nowadays it is conventional wisdom to *encourage* peasants to do precisely what their forefathers were fined or flogged for doing.

In much the same way, the system of agriculture derisively

known as slash and burn is now seen to be an exceedingly effective way of maximising output per person-hour of labour, and at the same time minimising the stress on the environment.

Even in the health field, once an area in which Western scientific thought was assumed to have an unassailable dominance, the skills of certain types of local doctors (again dismissively characterised as 'witch doctors' and often persecuted by the medical missionaries), and particularly their intimate knowledge of the healing properties of plants, is finally being recognised. In China, for example, so-called traditional medicine exists side by side with science-based medicine. The patient may choose which form of cure he or she prefers, or a health worker may suggest that for this particular complaint a scientific drug is indicated, while for that one chewing a specific root is the preferred treatment.

It was indeed in health care that modernisation theory had both the most dramatic and most laughable results. Starting with the premise that health care systems must be modernised, huge resources were poured into constructing modern hospitals with the full complement of state of the art medical gadgetry. I remember, for instance, visiting a leading Church hospital in India, and seeing a body-scanner there at a time when such technology had been available for only two or three years. Within three miles of this glory of modern medical technology there were villages with no access to clean water and where the Harijans (the Untouchables) were lucky to get work for a hundred days a year at minimal agricultural wages.

Were all projects undertaken by the Church agencies so tainted by modernisation thinking? And if they were, does it follow that all were as poor as this example? Luckily the answer to both questions is surely no. Many projects, especially large ones, were disappointing in their effects, frequently due to a mismatch between the perceptions of the project planner (often conditioned by modernising thinking) and the real needs of the people who were supposed to benefit from the project. That mismatch is not, however, inevitable. The closer the project initiator was to the intended beneficiaries, and the freer he felt to consult and carry the people with him, the greater the chance of success.

Furthermore, there *is* a grain of truth in the modernisation approach. Sometimes new approaches to problems are required. Western science and technology do have a role to play. Institutions do sometimes need radical overhaul. The difficulties arise when reality is perceived exclusively through Western perspectives, for then much of the reality of the poor is either missed altogether or misunderstood. In one little project in one village, that may not be a matter of too much moment. A latrine built by a Church-related donor goes unused because it is culturally unacceptable – or, in one case I know of personally, assumed to be put there solely for the use of visiting white dignitaries. Farming techniques remain 'backward' because the ones promoted by an agricultural project are observed by the farmers to be too risky in a year of low rainfall. A credit union collapses because its originators did not understand the processes of decision-making in the village. Aggregate these failures, these disappointments, and two reactions become endemic. Those on the receiving end of these projects become aware that they are being used, manipulated, not taken seriously as human beings with their own understanding of their own reality. And those on the giving end become frustrated that their good intentions are so frequently thwarted by the perverse, foolish or irrational attitudes of those they are trying to help.

There are here two further points which need to be classified further. First, modernisation theory implies that it is the low-income society that needs to be changed if living standards are to rise. The problem, in other words is 'out there', and change must take place 'out there'. Clearly this view ignores the impact of 'right here' on what is happening, can happen 'out there'. Indeed, it assumes that the metropolitan countries, the rich nations, can only have a *beneficial* impact (through example, aid and technology). The fact that through trade, investment, the communication of inappropriate consumption patterns and technologies the rich countries may be highly *destructive* of 'traditional' societies, or *obstructive* of the necessary changes, is either ignored or denied by modernisation theory.

Such theory therefore offers a sophisticated variety of scapegoating. It is 'their fault' that the poor countries (or poor people in poor countries) are 'backward'. The remedy lies in their own hands. If they refuse to modernise their attitudes and institutions, no guilt can be laid at the door of the rich nations.

Secondly, a 'modernising' approach to development encouraged the agencies (and, on a much larger scale, official aid institutions) to identify development with projects – projects to train, to educate, to build institutions, to improve technology, to upgrade agricultural methods, to organise this co-operative or that woman's group. Certainly, the missions had run projects and in that sense there was nothing new in a project approach. What was new was the saturation of many parts of 'easier' countries with projects, usually totally uncoordinated and all highly demanding in terms of administrative support and supervision. As we shall see there were powerful institutional forces pushing the agencies into this project-dominated style of work, but perhaps the most potent force of all was the basic definition of the notion of development. Modernisation theory implies that, given enough successful projects, development will be achieved. It does not encourage us to enquire about *process* – processes of enrichment and impoverishment, of participation and exclusion, of access and control. It thus diverts our attention from questions that are necessarily political and directs it exclusively to technocratic questions about the implementation of projects.

Once well under way, however, the project-machine was nearly unstoppable.

It was unstoppable for a very simple reason. The Churches, supremely in Germany and America, but also in Canada, Australia, Sweden and Denmark and somewhat later in the UK and Ireland, had scented big money in development. So too, incidentally, had the World Council of Churches whose development agencies now became the money spinner for the whole of the ecumenical movement. The sources of this new money were dominated by government.

Although the constitutional niceties varied from country to country, the fundamentals were nearly universal. The voluntary sector as a whole, of which the Churches were a major component, claimed to offer a highly cost-effective way of disbursing aid. They claimed other advantages. It was said they were more innovative, more participative, more easily able to reach the people really in need, less bureaucratic, better at fostering local initiative, more responsive to local leadership and less susceptible to political manipulation. Some of these claims may well have been true, though the small amount of serious research encourages a certain scepticism and can produce at least as long a list of negative factors, some of which we shall review below.

Certainly from a government standpoint, collaboration with the Churches had much to commend it. Aid disbursed through Church development agencies was administratively simple for the government departments concerned. It was electorally popular. It brought political and diplomatic benefits on the cheap. In some cases, it gave disguised political leverage without incurring the odium of crude neo-colonialism. And, consciously or unconsciously, it brought the Churches' willing connivance in the geopolitical objectives of metropolitan power. A well-financed Church is not a critical Church.

Indeed the synergy was almost perfect. For as long as the Churches were feeding off the aid vote, they had every reason to press for a larger aid allocation. If the Treasury or the Finance Ministry was tempted to attack the aid budget, the Ministry of Overseas development (or its equivalent, such as the Canadian International Development Agency or the Swedish International Development Authority or the American Agency for International Development) knew it could rely upon the Churches to mobilise political opinion to resist such pressures. The bandwagon looked unstoppable.

A further dimension now needs to be sketched in. In most countries, the Church development agencies were not exclusively dependent upon government financing. To a greater or lesser extent – greater in the UK, lesser in Germany – the agencies depended upon public support. To acquire and maintain that public support they had to develop their own rhetoric of success. They had to project themselves as successful agents of social change. They needed a good story to tell, good projects to write up. Above all they needed to develop a style of addressing their subscribers and contributors in a way that would maximise their fund-raising capacity. The message had to be simple, clear, positive and hopeful. Above all it had to be non-threatening to the interests, life-style and self-understanding of the urban middle classes in an increasingly secular, industrialised society. 'Give us more money and we'll do the job. We'll feed the starving babies and maybe enable their parents to feed them,' was the message. To suggest, as some voices had in ecumenical fora as early as 1966, that the very wealth of the industrial middle classes derived in some measure from the poverty of the developing world was not good for fund-raising and therefore not good for the Church agencies.

At every level then, the Church agencies were caught. They were caught by the intellectual *Zeitgeist* into which they had inevitably bought. They were caught by their increasing dependencies on state money, and they were caught by the rhetoric and image they needed to project in order to ensure their own survival and growth.

Chapter 4

1 The Recipients

As we have already seen in outline, the commitment of the
Churches of the rich nations to development came at an
historically awkward moment for the Church in Africa and
Asia. For the latter was involved in a delicate, difficult and,
above all, slow transition from the status of a mission-Church,
with all that that implies in terms of dependence, inequality
and 'receiving', to an independent, autonomous Church with
its own ideas, its own vision of its failure, its own theological
perspectives, its own financial resources and its own personnel.
Clearly, such a statement needs qualification and local
adaptation. It was more true in general of the mainline
Protestant Churches than of the Roman Catholic Church, not
least because the various missionary orders had a degree of
autonomy that guaranteed great diversity of policy on
indigenisation. In the same way, some Western mission boards
tried to force the pace, while others did their best to slow it
down. I recall one ex-missionary at the headquarters of his
society fulminating against a request from a 'daughter Church'
to be allowed to sing their own songs in Church: 'Once you
start down that road,' he warned, 'you never know where it will
end. They could be demanding their own bishops next.'

Whatever the pace of the transition, however, the demands
of a modernising, project-dominated approach to development posed real difficulties for the Churches in Africa and
Asia. For if the Churches were going to 'do development' in
ways different to the missions, they needed to establish
machinery that would make that possible. And if they were
going to 'do development' in a way that was consistent with the
increasingly rigorous criteria of their government pay-masters,
that machinery must be sufficient to withstand the impact of

large sums of money (mindblowingly large by the standards of the indigenous Church), with its demand for professional standards of project identification, implementation and evaluation.

Given that the whole development effort was ecumenical (at least in the narrow sense of Protestant ecumenism), it is natural that the conduit through which Church development aid would flow was new ecumenical entities in the developing countries themselves. The symmetry looked both natural and sensible. The National Council of Churches of the United States or Canada or Britain or whatever raised money from their own Churches, received grants from government, and through their specialised agencies passed that money to the National Council of Churches of Kenya or Tanzania or Zambia. Those Councils of Churches would set up their own development departments, which would help member churches identify and implement suitable development projects.

Like so many devices that look rational and efficient on paper, in practice this arrangement has been bedevilled by problems so profound that the Churches soon found themselves in deep crisis and the most prophetic voices began calling for total withdrawal and dismantling by the late 1960s – and continue to do so with greater urgency.[1] We can look at the problems under five headings.

First, are Church agencies the best means of implementing that conception of development held by civil servants in metropolitan capitals and public relations consultants of Church development agencies? In other words, if you think development is all about irrigation pumps, new agricultural technology, the modernisation of technique and institutions, would you naturally choose weak, struggling, understaffed (but often very rapidly growing) Churches as significant implementers of that kind of development?

A case can be made in their favour. Unlike many other institutions in the developing world, the Churches are in touch with rural people, and, as a result are often trusted by them, more readily than, for example, agencies of the domestic government. The Churches have a considerable administrative infrastructure that reaches down to the most remote village. They have educated clergy and lay people with a strong sense of vocation and service. Financial probity is highly valued and therefore the occurrence of corruption and misappropriation is less frequent than in many other institutions.

Such arguments are valid and important, but they do not, of course, amount to an answer to the original question: Are the Churches of Africa designed to be implementers of this Western, 'modernising' conception of development? It is to the great credit of many Church leaders in Africa that they were sceptical from the outset. Some, of course, were seduced: indeed many were dazzled by the offer of huge sums of money, training overseas, the provision of large numbers of white experts and, perhaps most significant of all, the possibilities of patronage for favoured sons. Wiser minds, however, quickly saw the dangers. Instead of having the whole life of the Church dominated by 'development', they wanted to keep it as a separate entity which would serve 'the real needs of the Church', as they saw them, rather than dictate or dominate those needs.

The idea, then, was to set up specialist development arms of National Councils of Churches which would absorb some of the threatening pressures of overseas aid, but which would still serve the Church's legitimate opportunities to witness to the Gospel by enabling the people to help themselves. This brings us to the second set of difficulties.

For it can hardly be claimed that these specialist development institutions have become effective implementers of modernisation notions of development. This may sound a harsh judgment and so it is as well to pay tribute to the hard work, energy, imagination and dedication that many people working in these institutions have brought to bear. The fact that the results have been so unsatisfactory is not a consequence of their failings. The issues go much deeper.

Let us leave aside undoubted deficiencies in training, staffing, administrative support, mobility, and technical competence. There is hardly a secular development agency in the Third World of which the same criticisms could not be made. Such problems are a continuously encountered symptom of poverty and have to be accepted and worked round if one is in this kind of business. The real issue lies in a fundamental mismatch at the heart of the modernisation paradigm. Precisely because the Churches are in contact with rural people – and for that matter poor people in the towns –

they are uncomfortable about dictating to the people what they need. The crude expert-dominated development-by-project-imposed-from-above has seldom been the style of the Churches in the developing countries. The paradox is that the more responsive the agencies are to the real needs, the needs articulated by the people, the more difficult it becomes to dress up those needs as the kind of project that the Church donor agencies are prepared to fund, or that they can sell to government agencies. Let me illustrate.

The Turkana of Northern Kenya have long been resistant to outside influences in general and 'development' in particular. When a representative of the ecumenical development network met with a group of Turkana he talked to them about the benefits to be derived from schools, health clinics and boreholes. Always courteous, the Turkana listened to him patiently. True to their belief, the representative emphasised that it was not for him to impose these great benefits upon them: he was there to listen to their priorities so that he could help them most effectively. There were of course, he told them, advantages in an integrated approach. If they had a school, the school would need a water supply: that could be extended to serve neighbouring villages and provide watering points for their cattle. People would come together and therefore a health clinic could provide preventive medicine and limited treatment for some of the simpler complaints. But, he repeated, it was for the Turkana to decide... The Turkana talked among themselves and after a long debate addressed the representative. 'We thank you for making this long journey to see us and share our problems. We have talked about it among ourselves. We have seen the effects of schools amongst other people. We do not want them. Water we need, but God gives us water. We have our own doctors. They know us and we know them. You have offered us nothing that we want. What we want is a place to bury our dead.'

I realise that this is an extreme, one might almost say odd, example. But the point it makes is crucial. Poor people in poor countries do not naturally think in terms of projects. They do not naturally think in the bureaucratically convenient categories of aid agencies and government finance officers. The truer one seeks to be to their perspectives, the priorities, their understanding of their own situation, the more difficult it becomes to design the kind of neat, hard-edged, time-bound project so beloved of the development industry. The difficulties that the ecumenical development arms of National Councils of Churches in Africa and elsewhere have encountered stem essentially from this mismatch between a project approach to development, required by the administrative and financial structures of the donors, and the process orientation of real people in real situations. I shall have more to say about this problem later.

Third the new development arms of National Councils of Churches quickly generated a life of their own. They were disposing of such huge sums of money – different orders of magnitude to the total operating budget of many member Churches of the national councils – that it became increasingly hard to see them as just another division of a Council of Churches. The division of mission and evangelism, for example, might employ four or five people; the division of women and youth might employ two or three; the development division would employ hundreds. Two possible results invariably ensued.

Kenya is a good example of the first. There, the development division was controlled by a tough-minded and politically adroit Kikuyu who soon made it clear that his activities were not to be constrained or controlled by the member Churches of the Council. Essentially, he opted for a separation of the ecumenical development effort from the life of the Church. Although much maligned for doing so, he was in fact (though perhaps unwittingly) following the example of the ecumenical donors, who were also becoming increasingly prone to slough off the control of the Church in the metropolitan countries.

The other result, perhaps most tragically illustrated in India, was that Church leaders sought to control the activities of the ecumenical development arm, in order to ensure that their own denominational interests were well served by the agency concerned. This inevitably led to conflict, confusion and contusion as individual Church leaders battled amongst themselves for what they saw as a fair share of the cake. It hardly needs saying that such institutionalised conflict did little to forward the cause either of ecumenism or of modernisation.

Lastly, and perhaps most obviously, the evolution of a large development bureaucracy in the National Councils of

Churches in poor countries became increasingly expensive and decreasingly efficient. In that it is no different from many secular agencies. Much more damagingly, however, the burgeoning bureaucracy generated a new breed of Church related development workers who were decreasingly in touch with the rural and urban poor whom they were supposed to serve. It is startling to contrast the styles and attitudes of Church development workers between, let us say, 1965 and 1980.

In East and Central Africa, for instance, in 1965, the few Church development workers in evidence were people who had lived and worked in the villages for most of their lives. They may not have been well educated and they were in no sense technical development experts. They were, however, extremely good at listening, at interpreting what was going on in the village, at understanding personal and political stresses and strains, at detecting where movement was possible, at taking things at a pace that the villagers could understand and make their own. Above all they respected, and I think it not too romantic to say loved, village life and villagers.

Fifteen, twenty years later those people have largely retired and although what they stood for remains, it remains only in vestigial form. Much of the new leadership is well (and often Western) educated, expert, articulate, competent, energetic and ambitious. This generation is urban in its aspirations, in its attitudes, in its background. It incorporates all the virtues that the moderniser values. The costs, however, are very high – and in the end they are paid by the poor in the villages.

The paradox is stunning. What the Churches had to offer was a sensitive understanding of the village – and is to a lesser extent of urban poor. That asset was seized and exploited – and destroyed. No doubt to say this is to generalise. Of course one can find outstanding individuals, occasionally outstanding groups of individuals working together, who still reflect and mediate the real needs of real people. It is, however, becoming rarer. The volume of money, the values of bureaucracy, the need to be or appear to be professional, the constant exposure to the demands of the donors for tidy projects, well written reports of success – all these are in the process of destroying the one asset the Church had to offer, closeness to the poor.

2 Modernisation and Theology

I have tried to describe the effect of a secular intellectual fashion on the worldwide ecumenical community in the 1950s, 1960s and 1970s. I have described it first in terms of what was going on in the metropolitan countries, and I want to conclude this chapter by pulling that together, in order to demonstrate the theological inadequacy of the Church's ready swallowing of the modernisation paradigm. One of the oddities of the whole story is that the modernisation paradigm was never subjected to serious theological critique. Indeed, the theological work undertaken by the development agencies is most noticeable for its absence or low quality. For the development activists regarded theology as irrelevant.

The tragedy is that, given the kind of theology that was being written and debated in most metropolitan countries, they were quite right. It had to wait for various strands of thought that are usually lumped under the umbrella of liberation theology to appear – significantly, from the developing world itself – before theology had anything significant to say concerning what was going on.

For the rest, theological effort was confined to convincing Christians in the metropolitan countries that they had a duty to their neighbours in the developing world. That, of course, served the interests of the development agencies. By playing on guilt and representing themselves as ways by which that guilt could be expunged, they were able to generate a new level of giving. Theology had once again become the lap-dog of the prevailing ideology.

We shall have to return to this theme later. For the moment an example will bring out what I want to communicate. Everyone knows the intense suffering of the people of Uganda under Idi Amin. When he was finally overthrown Uganda prepared itself – ironically as history proved – for a return to peace and normality. As part of that process, the Anglican Church in Uganda (the largest Protestant Church in the country) drew up a ten year development plan under the able leadership of Bishop Cyprian Bamwoze of Jinja. It was a comprehensive document that incorporated the newly conventional wisdom of a holistic approach to Church development and the development of people.

The plan, as finally ratified by the Church of Uganda, included everything from pig farms to the reprinting of the Church in Uganda hymn books. There were many institutional projects, in the sense of repairing and upgrading schools and hospitals that had suffered during the preceding ten years. There were also requests for rebuilding the living accommodation of the clergy, much of which had been destroyed. There was even a request for replacing cassocks and surplices that had simply vanished during Amin's atrocities in the villages. There was, as I have already implied, also a large number of conventional 'development' projects from training farms to vocational schools.

This impressive document was circulated to the main Church donor agencies in the metropolitan countries. Ever on the lookout for fundable projects, the agencies were soon able to promise funding for development projects. The institutional projects took longer, but with a certain amount of arm twisting and explanation most of them were eventually covered. Progress then slowed to a standstill. I shall never forget meeting Bishop Bamwoze when it had become clear to him what was happening.

'Your people,' he said 'have a very strange idea of the Gospel. They will pay for housing for pigs but not for priests. They will pay for the printing of maths books but not for hymn books. They will rebuild schools but not Churches. They will train mechanics, but not ministers. Is this then the Gospel of the Western Churches? You will feed the body but not the soul? Is that what you think of the Kingdom of God – that it is a kind of universal Marks and Spencers? Come now, how can I go to my people in the villages and say that our friends in Europe want us to keep pigs but don't want us to sing our beloved songs? How can I tell them that they are free to buy Landrovers for the diocesan development officers but they can't even buy a bicycle for the catechist? Do you know what they will say to me? They will say to me: "Ha, Bishop; you are bringing us Western materialism, not the Christian faith".'

That, of course, is precisely the point. Notions of development based upon the modernisation paradigm are open to all the objections to Western materialism, for modernisation is implicitly – and sometimes quite explicitly – an invitation to ape the West. The West is *defined* as modern and the developing world as traditional, primitive. The process of modernisation then is the process of transition from the 'primitive' to the Western. Largely unconsciously, the Western Churches had become the agents by which Western materialism, Western modernism, was to be transferred to the developing world. Direct imperialism had been replaced by cultural imperialism and the Churches had allowed themselves to become its unwitting agents. No wonder Bishop Bamwoze was angry.

Yet there is another paradox in this state of affairs. For by the early 1960s all the Churches, Protestant and Roman Catholic, were becoming increasingly critical of many of the features of European and North American life which were appearing on the back of the post-war boom. It was not just a question of rising rates of divorce, suicide, alcoholism, child abuse and all the familiar symptoms of anomie and stress in a high consumption society. Nor was it merely a first flicker of what came to be known as the Green Revolt. It went deeper than either of those reactions. Thinkers like Roszak, Marcuse and Ellul, poets like Eliot; novelists like Wilson, playwrights like Osborne – all were reflecting a deep existential unease about a civilisation that had lost its way. Nor were the best theological minds unaware of this crisis. In very different terms, Branner, Tillich and Moltmann all reflected it. What explains, then, the failure of the Church's development activists to reflect more critically upon the value systems with which they were operating – and which they were transferring?

3 The Agencies Trapped

There is no single answer to that question: two features, however, seem significant. The first is that the Church development agencies in the metropolitan countries became victims of their own processes. That is to say, they were trapped both by their dependence on the state and the increasingly affluent middle classes for their money. Perhaps even more importantly, they became dependent upon the development bureaucracies they had helped to create in the developing world. They needed those bureaucracies if they were to identify enough neatly packaged projects to spend their growing budgets. By the mid-1970s, however, these bureaucracies were becoming adept at producing such projects – and knew they had to do so in order to survive. A kind of symbolic relationship emerged between the metropolitan development agencies (which needed to spend money) and the recipient organisations (which had to play the game by the rules of the metropolitan agencies).

Underneath this symbiosis lay a second and much more sinister factor. Caught in the project dance, neither the agencies in the metropolitan countries nor the so-called recipient institutions in the developing world were in a structural position to ask the key question that, late in the 1970s, became the title of a best-selling book: Why poor people stay poor.[2] Modernisation theory virtually assumes this question away. Poor people stay poor because they are backward, stupid, lazy, disorganised and incompetent. As a serious answer to the fundamental question, that is of course, wholly inadequate.

Poor people stay poor for a vast array of reasons, one of the most significant of which, as I shall argue in more detail later, is that they are caught in a web of relationships that deprive them of any wealth above the most meagre subsistence. Those relationships spread out from the village through the towns into the international economy.

Furthermore, those relationships are interconnected – that is to say, there is a connection between the international dimension and the domestic dimension. In that sense both the metropolitan powers (represented in this discussion by the Churches in the metropolitan countries) and the urban élites (represented by the development professionals in the recipient organisations) are involved in maintaining poor people in their poverty.

Now, if one conceives of development as essentially the process of putting together the right bundle of projects to transform rural and eventually urban society, one is prevented from seeing how this network of relationships maintains poverty. If poverty persists, it is, one supposes, because insufficient projects or the wrong bundles of projects have been implemented. The remedy is more projects, more money, more professionals, more agencies. The fundamental relationships of power and wealth extraction are simply never faced.

The point is this. The metropolitan Church development agencies were not in a position to face those kinds of questions, even though they were being raised by the 'thinking' parts of the ecumenical community. The agencies could not adequately confront those questions, not only because they lacked the expertise or intellectual fire power[3] – but also because they were trapped both by their constituency (their contributors), and by their reliance on heavy government funding. For to face the full implications of a quite different development paradigm would have brought them into sharp conflict with government – and with the economic and political interests of the majority of people from whom they were raising their money. Furthermore, in some countries at least, Councils of Churches had come to depend upon their development agencies for *their own* funding. Thus as recently as 1985, the British Council of Churches decided that it would levy one percent of the income of its development arm to defray the recurrent costs of the council. Given the great growth of income on the back of the Ethiopian appeal, the Council's finances were transformed at a stroke. Needless to say, this deft manoeuvre was not widely publicised.

It is important to get the nuance of the argument right. I am not suggesting that evil people in the development agencies deliberately suppressed new understandings that were, in the early 1970s, becoming available about the development process. Nor am I suggesting that they were so craven or corrupt that they ignored the truth as they saw it. Instead I am suggesting that they were structurally unable to adapt to new perspectives, fresh challenges.

This fact should not be surprising. All institutions develop a life of their own and become comfortable with a particular view of the world, a defined set of procedures, an established network of relationships. It is a most unusual institution that can, as it were, adopt a new persona, a new self-understanding so that it operates in a new way. Institutional life contains something akin to the pattern of evolution. A particular institution is well adapted to a particular environment and a particular set of objectives. When environment and objective change, the institution does not have the capacity to adapt and therefore ultimately (often after a very long delay) collapses. We should not be surprised or offended, therefore, that a set of ecclesiastical arrangements that was born out of the one world view, and which became well adapted to the set of objectives and procedures indicted by that world view, should not have within it the capacity to adapt to a different world view. It would have been astonishing, almost miraculous, if it had had that capacity.

It did not. And it does not. It survives. The project system survives. The relationships that I have described, with both their strengths and their weaknesses, continue. But the game moves on. We see that illustrated dramatically at the heart of the ecumenical family. By 1970 a coalition of those who were increasingly unhappy with the assumptions and procedures of the Church donor agencies came together to mount a major assault on their thinking and policies. That coalition comprised a number of representatives of Third World Church agencies – mostly younger, more 'radical', often Eastern educated; a contingent of Latin American social scientists, some of whom had been exiled by military régimes in their own countries; some younger people from the rich country donor agencies who had begun to read Latin American critiques of modernisation theory; and a core of officials of the World Council of Churches who were angered by what they saw as the insensitive use of power by the larger Church agencies, especially the American and German ones.

The outcome was predictable. A new ecumenical entity was established by the World Council of Churches as a focus for the new thinking. To divert some of the anger and criticism they had received, many of the larger donors gave some financial support to this new creation, the Commission on the Church's Participation in Development. It has to be said, however, that there was more than a tinge of Chinese opera about the proceedings. Within two years, the sting of the challenge of CCPD had been drawn. The donors were a little more aware, a little more sensitive, a little more cautious, but the structural and ideological positions remained little changed. Although it produced some excellent work, of which we shall have more to say later, CCPD slowly withered in influence, in innovative ideas and, most sadly, in power to subject the donors to theological critique.

The project dance continues...

Chapter 5

1 The Justice Challenge to Modernisation

As we have already seen, from the earliest ecumenical debates on development, there were those who wanted to cast the debate in terms of justice rather than modernisation. By 1970, this issue had become so fiercely contested that the World Council of Churches could handle it only in the same way as the United Nations – itself a parallel that is as revealing as it is paradoxical – that is to say, by setting up another institution to work on justice issues, while leaving the well-established 'modernisation' institutions intact. In the case of the UN, the Conference on Trade and Development (UNCTAD) had been established in 1963, at the insistence of the poor countries to offset the domination of the major 'donor' institutions such as the World Bank, and of the 'rich man's club' image of the GATT.[1]

Now, seven years on, the ecumenical community found itself going down the same track, with the Commission on the Churches' Participation in Development set up to offset the donors' club at the WCC. Perhaps nothing speaks to eloquently of the power of an ideology and the interests grouped around it than that the Churches could find no other way to deal with the challenge of justice than to hive it off into its own institutional cocoon – a feature mirrored at many levels of the Churches' life, right down to the parish or congregation. Why did the justice issues represent such a threat? It is that question which we shall explore in this chapter.

Justice is a chameleon word to which it is notoriously difficult to attach a precise meaning, or rather to which precise meanings are attached by the total context in which the word is used. For our purposes, the chameleon-like quality of the word is particularly important, since it helps to explain the way in which different schools of thought and ideological positions have become confused and intertwined in the process of the Church's work in development – often with unsatisfactory and sometimes with disastrous results.

It will be no surprise to discover that the initial progenitors of a vocabulary of justice were those who felt that they were not getting justice. For me personally this has always been best symbolised by a demonstration of young Africans at the Uppsala Assembly of the World Council of Churches. One of the placards, carried by a fully robed Nigerian, read 'Justice Not Charity'. There are many strands of thought here, but we shall disentangle three at this stage.

First, that demonstration was against a style of development that smacked of rich man's philanthropy, which is how the modernisation paradigm looked – and continues to look – to many in the developing world. The rich Christians, the rich Churches, rich nations, were prepared to give charitably of their abundance; they were not prepared to look critically at the economic and political structures which kept poor people poor, and which ensured that the major beneficiaries of their charitable giving were the non-poor.

A second strand was a challenge to the process of decision making *within* the modernisation paradigm. In this sense the demand for justice was a demand for a more open, transparent style within the donor/recipient relationship in the Churches *and* a similar style between donor and recipients at the national or secular levels. To this extent, the justice paradigm has heavy overtones of what later came to be identified as the demand for participation – itself another chameleon word, but one which encapsulated the resentments in the developing world against a style which assumed that the rich knew what was best for the poor. This assumption is itself an outgrowth of the modernisation paradigm, since if the process of development is essentially recreating Western structures, Western values, Western social processes, it follows that those who have been brought up in a Western culture are in a better position to transfer those features of their own culture.

Third, the justice theme developed early, lost and then refound an overtone of reparation. That is to say, many in the developing world saw justice as demanding not charity, which was equated with tokenism, but a serious attempt to right the wrongs – at least in a financial sense – that had been wrought by colonialism and, as it was alleged, by neo-colonialism. If the political model was the reparations paid by the defeated countries after World Wars I and II, the theological model was that of the jubilee in which slaves are freed, debts cancelled and pledges annulled (Lev. 25:9-10). The argument was that the rich and powerful had used their wealth and power in a way that made poverty inevitable, and that justice could only be done by the rich repairing the social fabric that they were destroying.[2]

It is immediately apparent that two senses in which the word justice was used in ecumenical development circles were to varying degrees compatible with the modernisation paradigm. One sense in which it was used concerned decision making within that paradigm; another sense underlined the scale of transfers to be made. If the latter left open the question of the ways in which those transferred resources would be deployed, the usual assumption was that they would be used in ways that were consistent with modernisation thinking.

It was only the first sense – contrasting structural change with modernisation – that really posed a serious philosophical and ultimately theological threat to modernisation thinking. Much of this chapter will therefore concentrate on the ways in which that threat was deployed and the reasons why it has been largely unsuccessful.

2 Structuralism

In the secular world, the modernisation paradigm came under severe attack first and most persuasively from Latin America.[3] A group of Latin American economists and sociologists, associated with the United Nations Economic Commission for Latin America based in Santiago in Chile, subjected the assumptions and implications of modernisation theory to a searching critique. The core of their argument was that it was simply fallacious to assume that Latin America was poor because it lacked Western types of institutions. They argued that such an assumption misread the history of Latin America and misunderstood present day reality in that continent.

For, they argued, Latin America had regularly demonstrated its capacity for industrialisation, agricultural change and efficient bureaucracy but, over and over again, these possibilities had been thwarted by influences from overseas. Whenever Latin American exports, for example, became competitive and capable of challenging entrenched interest in the rich countries, they were kept out by protectionist measures or direct political interference. Foreign investors, particularly from the United States, it was claimed, continually sucked out of Latin America more capital than they put in, thus permanently impoverishing the continent.

These criticisms were not confined to international relations. It was argued, for example, that a long-standing conflict between land owners and industrialists, itself fought out in the domestic political arena, had resulted in exchange rate policies that made permanent economic advance impossible. Even within the agricultural sector itself the role of absentee land owners, sometimes owning farms as big as the principality of Wales, had made agricultural progress impossible.

The common element that bound these social scientists together was their insistence on the importance of structures. These structures might be political, they might be legal, they might be economic, they might be sociological. In the most penetrating analyses, structures at all these levels were shown to interact to make the elimination of poverty impossible. Because of the centrality of the notion of structure, these thinkers came to be called structuralists. Although one particular form of structural analysis came to dominate secular thinking in the form of dependency theory, it is hard to over-estimate the significance of structural analysis in pinpointing key areas where notions of justice became clamant. An illustration will help clarify this point.

Perhaps one of the most important contributions of structural thinking, associated with the names of Raoul Prebisch of ECLA and Hans Singer latterly of the Institute of Development Studies at Sussex University, was the observation that there are powerful economic reasons for expecting the commodity exports of developing countries to buy less and less manufactured goods from the industrialised countries.[4] The details of the theory need not detain us here. Essentially the argument is that demand for most commodity exports – coffee, cotton, cocoa, copper, lead, zinc, groundnuts, timber –

grows only slowly in the developed countries, while their supply (particularly of agricultural commodities) increases as more and more countries start to produce them. Further, the way these commodities are sold (essentially at an international auction that clears the market) contrasts with the way in which tractors or turbines are sold – on a cost plus basis, where costs incorporate a given standard of living for all who produce those tractors and turbines. These two basic asymmetrics explain, said Singer and Prebisch, why the purchasing power of the exports of developing countries seems constantly to be eroded.[5] The *structures* of international trading arrangements ensure that wealth is extracted from the developing country commodity producers and passed to the rich industrialised countries.

It is clearly but a small step to move from that observation to a justice vocabulary. It is unjust, it might well be argued, that the rich countries keep in being an international trading system that enables them to build into the structures of international trade a comfortable standard of living for themselves, while they deny that possibility to their ex-colonial suppliers of raw materials.

In much the same way, it is possible to apply a justice vocabulary to many of the basic arguments that emerged from the Latin American structuralists in the late 1950s and 1960s. It is unjust, for example, that some individuals own but do not develop large tracts of land while the majority of the rural population seeks to eke out a living on tiny parcels of land. Land reform is not only a question of efficiency: it is a question of equity, of justice.

The same logic can be applied to social goods like education and health care. Structuralists argue that the provision of education and health care is structured in a way that makes it very difficult for the poor to get a fair share, or even any share at all, of these services. Poor families cannot afford to send their children to school, even if the school is free,[6] for the family depends upon the earnings of the child. Health services tend to be concentrated in urban areas, where health-care resources are gobbled up by expensive high-tech hospitals, with the result that even basic preventative care of the rural population gets squeezed out of the budget.[7] The structuralists' explanation of the unequal distribution of access to education and health was easily translated into justice language. It is unjust that the urban middle classes have access to high quality thoracic surgery while the urban poor go unprotected from malaria and measles. It is unjust that in Kenya the son of an urban civil servant is 700 times more likely to finish secondary school than the son of a peasant farmer.[8]

Structuralism, however, goes deeper than this. The social-science-based structuralism of Prebisch, Cardoso and Laclau is related to the philosophical and linguistic structuralism that had a major impact in the United States of America and Europe. Instead of looking at structures of society, it was shown to be important to look at structures of thought, structures of language, structures of meaning. Why do we think the way we do and why do we accept one explanation for a given phenomenon while rejecting another explanation? What is it that gives some words in our vocabulary resonance, depth, the power to illuminate and motivate while other words have the capacity to turn us off? Contrast, for instance, the way in which we respond to the word 'democracy', with the way in which we respond to the phrase 'one party state'.

The implications of this brand of structuralism are profound, raising questions that were implicit in the social science formulations of structuralism, but giving them a harder edge and greater penetration. Essentially they turn out to be questions about power. That is to say they are questions about which groups in society determine how language, explanation and meaning are constructed and used.[9] They therefore raise a whole new generation of perspectives on development and justice, and it is in that context that we shall have to return to them.

Let us confine the argument for the moment, then, to the rather less daunting brand of thinking that denies the simple assumptions of modernisation theory and insists that explanations for the persistence of poverty have to be sought amongst the international and national structures that create and maintain poverty. How did the Church development community respond to this type of thinking?

3 The Church's reponse to Structuralism

It is immediately obvious, surely, that structuralism poses a challenge to Churches in both rich and poor countries. For once the basic hypothesis is granted – that poverty is created and maintained by the *structure* of society – the Church is challenged at three levels. First, the Church itself is a structure in society, and as such controls a wide range of institutions (or structures), particularly in education and health care. Second, it might be argued that if the Church is to take the demand for justice seriously, it has to be prepared to contend with, that is bring into contention, unjust structures in society over which the Church itself has no control (for example, the international trading system). Third, the Church has to identify and ally itself with alternative structures that seem to have less evil consequences for the poor. In what senses was the Church able to respond to these three levels of challenge?

In terms of the Church's own structures, it was clear that the Church, in both rich countries and poor, had large assets. Structuralist thinking brought the nature and use of these assets under scrutiny. How, for instance, was the Church using its wealth? How was the Church using its land? What was the effect of Church schools and hospitals on the distribution of health and education?

Under the influence of the Conferences of Medellin and Puebla, many Roman Catholic bishops, especially in Latin America, began to re-examine the inherited wealth of the Church, particularly in terms of land, and ask whether it should not be used in quite different ways. In the Caribbean, for example, some of the bishops made over their land to groups of young people to farm as co-operatives. In Brazil, Cardinal Arns courted the charge of communism (with all the legal implications that such a charge carried in Brazil in the 1970s) because he made Church property available to the base communities, to use as they saw fit.

The example was contagious. In the United States a number of religious Orders began to make available property to disadvantaged groups with the very minimum of supervision and control. Even in the United Kingdom, in riot-torn Brixton the Church of England made over a showpiece church to the local community, dominated by Afro-Caribbeans, to provide them with a community centre. Many such examples could be cited and it is not part of my purpose to belittle or deprecate the courageous and costly steps that were taken.

It is important however, to set these courageous gestures in context. First, with the possible exception of land reform, this reassignment of assets made very little impact on the structural position of the whole Church in society, and even less on the way that the structures of that society create and maintain poverty in both rich countries and poor. Second, the scale of the reallocation of assets to poor people was and remains tiny in proportion to the total value of assets controlled by the Church. The figures cannot refute the charge of tokenism.

Another indicator of the Church's reaction to structuralist thinking is afforded by the Church's stewardship of its investments. It would be too easy but misleading to say that structuralist thinking made no impact on this area. In the United States, for example, from the early 1970s onwards, a series of increasingly articulate and expert lobbies has been trying to persuade the Churches to revise their investment strategies.

Initially starting with fairly traditional criteria about the ethics of investment – e.g. hostility to investments in armaments firms, known exploiters of Third World labour and destroyers of the environment – the ethics of investment debate soon moved into much deeper water, raising questions about the ethics of the Church living on profits from the capitalist system at all. If the Church had to own accumulated capital (and that question became increasingly open to debate through the 1970s and 1980s, even in some major denominations of the United States and particularly in some Catholic Orders) should it not be investing in forms of economic organisations that offered alternatives to capitalism?[10]

By comparison with such profound questions, it was almost with relief that the Churches faced the more manageable question of disinvestment from companies with major subsidiaries in South Africa; from companies heavily involved in producing export crops (e.g. bananas in Central Africa, pineapples in the Philippines); mining companies in the developing world that were suspected of racist employment policies or using too much leverage on their host governments to reduce their tax burden; or companies that ignored UN norms, and particularly sanctions against Zimbabwe.

It is, however, once again important to put this whole debate into context. The amount of money reinvested as a result of these kinds of consideration was relatively small in the United States. In the UK it was negligible. Only in Holland did some of the Churches and the religious orders take these issues sufficiently seriously to review the whole pattern of the Church's assets. Even there it is still a moot point whether the new pattern of investment reflected an adequate response to the structuralist critique.

It was on the Church as a provider of education and health services that the full weight of the structuralist critique came to bear – both overseas, and, increasingly, in the metropolitan countries themselves. It is important to emphasise, however, that those calling into question the conventional Church provision of comfortable facilities for the comfortable classes were not necessarily using the language of the structuralist critique of modernisation theory. Medellin, Puebla and much of the writing of the liberation theologians all reflected that critique. It is significant, however, that the debate had started and indeed begun to take effect before these ecclesiastical fora began to adopt the ideas and approaches of the structuralists.

Health care is a particularly interesting case in point. It was one of the few areas in which there was genuine collaboration between the Protestant ecumenical family in the World Council of Churches and the Roman Catholic Church. The Christian Medical Commission, with its headquarters in the WCC building in Geneva, incorporated staff from Roman Catholic Orders who were beginning to call into question (as early as 1968) the heavy curative – 'disease-palace' – pattern of health care provided by Church agencies. And this was not all – the CMC was also using its considerable influence actively to *prevent* Churches and Church agencies from building such hospitals in the developing world, if necessary by persuading Government Health Departments to withhold permission. By gaining a foothold in the World Health Organisation whose officers by some stroke of serendipity were within 500 yards of those of the World Council, the Christian Medical Commission was able to both use the authority of the World Health Organisation for its own stance, and simultaneously to persuade the World Health Organisation to give much greater emphasis – and ultimately resources – to primary health care.

The story is, of course, much more complicated than that: it is interesting to speculate, for example, how far the booming fashion of primary health care in the 1970s was a result of cold political calculation by the politicians who control the World Health Organisation through its assembly. There are more votes in a thousand primary health care clinics in the rural areas than there are in a cardiac ward in the main hospital in the capital. The latter may be popular with the élite, but the former will be popular with the rural masses. Be that as it may, it is a fact of chronology that the Church's ecumenical response to the structuralist critique of health care led to an important development in the international politics of health.

However, once again one needs to ask how much difference does it make at the grass roots? How many Church hospitals were closed down in order to release resources for preventive care in the rural areas and in the urban slums? The history of the Vellore Medical College in South India is an interesting example in this respect.

Vellore is one of the premier medical schools in India and the most prestigious, high-quality Church medical school in the Indian sub-continent. The kind of thinking I have been describing did not leave Vellore untouched. By the early 1970s Indian Christians were asking whether it was appropriate that Vellore should be producing extremely well-educated doctors who would settle into comfortable practices in the major Indian cities and become part, albeit a Christian part, of the urban super-élite. Was there not something repugnant to the Christian conscience, it was asked, about a Christian college producing generations of doctors who would perform medical marvels for the rich, while leaving the vast majority of the Indian population, including many Christian poor, totally untouched by medical science?

In response to these questions, Vellore eventually, and at least in some quarters reluctantly, took the step of establishing an integrated project in a group of nearby villages that set primary health care in the widest context of agricultural development, village improvement and, rather less emphasised, political education. The initial plan was that all medical students at Vellore would spend a significant period of their training working in this project and learning at first hand the social reality faced by village India. The hope and expectation was that this would provide them with an insight that would develop into a vocation to devote their lives to bringing preventive health care to the rural poor, rather than following their predecessors to the greener pastures of the city suburbs.

The history of the project, in particular the history of the relationships between the project's directors and the authorities of the medical school, is sad, verging on tragic. Misunderstandings, jealousies, professional defensiveness, ideological suspicions, confusion and uncertainty all combined slowly to erode the original vision. By 1983 the cutting edge of that vision had been so blunted that it was no longer feasible to look to Vellore to effect the transformation of Christian medical work in India. The old value of professional élitism had re-established themselves.

Is the same picture – of a genuinely vigorous but in the end somewhat marginal attempt to respond to the structuralists' challenge – true in the case of education? The picture seems to be much more confused, much more piecemeal – perhaps inevitably so, given the vastly greater past investment in education and the complexity which is a feature of the organisation of the Church's educational services. Certainly one can find some early examples of the Church trying to respond to the structuralist challenge. Take the Loretto Sisters in Kenya, for example. An Order with an élitist style and tradition, immediately after independence it was running one of the best girls' secondary schools in Kenya. Perhaps rather late in the day, it had become multi-racial, attracting the daughters of the increasingly prosperous but numerically somewhat limited Kenyan élite, most of them Kikuyu. Jumping to the other end of the spectrum, the sisters started a vocational school in one of the most remote, backward and least hospitable areas of rural Kenya, using the 'profits' from the higher class school to subsidise the bush school. Roughly in between these extremes, they were running a school in Mombasa which sought to cater for a broader social spectrum. But the dilemma remains. Was it right to withdraw from the Nairobi school and thus run the risk of reducing the Christian influence on the ruling élite? On the other hand, was it right to allow the offspring of that élite to be cocooned in an educational system that isolated them from the realities of most of Kenya's poor? Could that particular Order, with its own traditions, with its complement of elderly white sisters and very few younger African sisters, aspire to engage in the new forms of education to which the structuralists' challenge pointed?

I take this example as typical of the dilemmas which have been facing many expatriate teaching institutions from the mid 1960s. The response to that dilemma, of course, varied greatly. Some middle class schools were closed down or handed over to the government or other secular bodies. Some teaching Orders withdrew entirely from the developing world. Some sought new patterns of ministry, particularly among what came to be called base communities.

It is arguable, however, that the greatest influence on the Church's involvement in education in the developing world over this period (from 1960-80) was not the challenge of structuralism, with its implied justice criteria, but the brute facts of money and government control. As I have already emphasised, newly independent governments, particularly in Africa, were anxious to seize control of the whole educational apparatus. Given the financial precariousness of the Churches, most were unable to resist. Paradoxically, indeed perversely, only the wealthier urban schools could be made sufficiently independent of government finance successfully to resist pressures for ceding control to the government. Redeployment of resources certainly occurred – and the structuralist/justice criteria coincided with that redeployment. Perhaps it made it easier and less threatening to let go of mainline education involvement when the time came. It would, however, be unhistorical to claim that it was justice criteria alone that changed the pattern of the Church's involvement in education over these twenty years.

4 The Church, Structuralism and the World

We must now leave the Church's response to the structuralist critique with respect to its own institutions and move to the more difficult ground of the Church's reaction to the same critique of secular structures. How far was the Church, in both rich and poor countries, able to respond to the argument that

COMFORTABLE COMPASSION? **63**

poverty is created and sustained by structures and structural relationships in society as a whole?

Let us consider the rich countries first. Structuralist thinking raised a number of uncomfortable questions. We have already mentioned one of the most central: the international trading system. There were, however, others: the international monetary system, foreign investment, the transfer of technology, access to information and the role of the military, the process of impoverishment at home which created and maintained a sub-class, often racially defined, of permanently poor, the victims of what the jargon came to call 'multi-deprivation'. Each of these represented huge, complex and deeply debated areas in which it was argued that the structures imposed by the rich played a part in the maintenance of the poverty of the poor. A moment's thought reveals that, as far as the international concession is concerned, each of these has far greater impact on the developing world in general and the living standards of poor people in particular than the international aid effort. As the economic history of Latin America in the 1980s was to reveal so starkly, a small change in the price of an export crop or a rise in interest rates on its overseas debt could far exceed the value of aid to a developing country. Exposure to the wrong technology could lose more jobs than aid could create and, by manipulating tastes and patterns of consumption, it could produce more hunger and malnutrition than aid could relieve.

Yet almost by definition these areas are beyond the technical competence or sphere of action of the Churches. Aid, the Church agencies know and understand – albeit within a wretchedly circumscribed mind-set. They can assess, however crudely, the quantity of aid made available by their domestic governments. These more technical structural issues pose a real problem. The clergy are not trained to understand them, and only a tiny handful of lay people are sufficiently close to them to be helpful. There is, however, a more significant and more insidious point. Many of those lay Christians who are involved in international trade or technology transfer or banking find it difficult to subject their area of daily concern – which also happens to be their source of daily bread – to the kind of radical critique that the proclamation of the Kingdom demands. It is not only that the relatively few Christians who are involved in these areas tend to be politically conservative. They also tend to see capitalism as a morally good, perhaps even divinely sanctioned, form of economic organisation. Within capitalism, they tend to regard the functioning of the market, whether for capital or technology or manufactured goods or raw materials, as the 'invisible hand' that guides human society to the greatest happiness of the greatest number.[11]

It is asking a very great deal – far more, I suspect, than many clergy and professional development lobbyists realise – of such people to make the perceptual leap from the snug commercial environment in which they are embedded, to the perspective of the Kingdom of God in which the rich and powerful are brought under judgment, and the Kingdom is proclaimed to the poor and the lowly and the meek.

That perspective is so far out with the normal mind-set of those who operate the structures that it is not hard to understand why most Churches most of the time have remained mystified at, confused by, and therefore negligent of the central issues involved. I have spoken many times so far in this book of the historical inevitability of much that now seems inadequate or unfortunate. Here I suggest we are confronting a sociological inevitability. The Church finds it hard to mobilise this kind of intellectual expertise among its professionals; those (lay) members of the Church who have the expertise are, for the most part, trapped in the very structures that need to be brought under judgment.

But is it as easy as that? If the Churches were able to mobilise secular professional expertise in the service of the modernisation paradigm, why were they unable to mobilise professional expertise to help them grapple with the admittedly difficult issues of structural injustice? Some attempts, of course, were made. The Vatican's Pontifical Commission for Justice and Peace, the American ecumenical lobby Bread for the World, the World Development Movement in the United Kingdom, and some of the more radical groups in Holland and Germany were, even as early as 1972, trying to get some of these issues on the Church's agenda.

A particularly significant early attempt was Marion Gallis's study of international trade, *Trade for Justice*. Published by the Commission on the Church's Participation in Development of the WCC in 1972, just prior to the third meeting of the

UN Conference on Trade and Development, it was hoped this report would influence both the UN and the Churches in the rich countries. There is little evidence of that hope being fulfilled, though the report did serve as useful ammunition for the voluntary agencies' fringe groups at the UNCTAD meeting in Chile.

In general, these attempts to put structures of trade on the agenda of the Churches ran into two difficulties. The first was the difficulty of mystification. The issues involved are not simple (although often the mechanisms behind them are surprisingly obvious) and it was therefore hard to communicate to 'ordinary Church people' the nature of the structural features that were being called into question. It was thus easy for those who had a different point of view, or a different set of interests, to accuse the Churches of simplification or indeed of simplicity.[12] The narrow path between simple-mindedness and incomprehensibility proved extremely difficult to find and follow.

Secondly, and perhaps more importantly, when Church people did begin to understand the ways in which, for example, asymmetrical trading practices remove wealth from the poor and transfer it to the rich, they were nonplussed. They felt powerless. Lacking both confidence in their own under-standing of the issues and an obvious lever by which those issues could be manipulated, they not unnaturally fell back on something they did understand, the volume of aid or disaster relief. The totemisation of 0.7 per cent of GNP – the UN target for the proportion of national income that should be devoted to aid – this became a refuge from both the complexities of the real world and from the sense of powerlessness in dealing with the real world.

None of this of course is to deny that Church assemblies, synods, conferences and committees, passed worthy resol-utions on many structural issues, nor that teams of Churchmen and women visited political representatives and members of government in all the rich countries with which I am familiar. Of course that happened. It is no exaggeration, however, to say that, in the terms of the debate as I have outlined them, they achieved virtually nothing. Indeed, they almost certainly achieved worse than nothing: they gave some of the Church people involved the impression that they were being taken seriously as they seriously addressed serious issues. On aid, they came to be taken perhaps half seriously; on trade I have found no evidence they had any impact at all.

The terms of trade issue is (nonetheless) an interesting illustration. In the period under review, there was one serious and one quarter-serious attempt to come to terms with the fact that the poor countries have, since 1951, found themselves in a situation where they have to export more and more raw materials to pay for a given quantity of manufactured imports. This is sometimes called the terms of trade problem. The major attempt to deal with this was launched by the United Nations Conference on Trade and Development in the mid-1970s, in the shape of proposals for the establishment of the so-called Common Fund.

The Common Fund was to be an internationally financed fund which would intervene in the free market of the eighteen commodities of most interest to poor countries. It was a *common* fund because its resources would be made available for intervention in each of the eighteen markets. That there were technical difficulties with this approach is not in dispute; and that it would have required vastly more resources than its promoters were prepared to admit has been proved by the passage of time.

Nor is it entirely true that the deep and at times passionate international debate on the establishment of the Common Fund was entirely neglected by the Churches. That would be unfair. It is, however, quite clear that at a time when America, Japan, Germany and Britain were doing their best to impede the progress of negotiations or neuter the provisions of the protocols of the Common Fund, the Churches were not a significant force challenging that political reaction. Contrast the role of the Churches on Sunday trading legislation in 1984-85 in the UK; or on school progress a little earlier in the US.

The other approach to the terms of trade problem that is worth a brief mention was the Brandt Report.[13] Particularly in the UK (in marked contrast to the United States) the Churches did take note of Brandt and consequently tried their best to extract from the Conservative Government in the United Kingdom a more positive and constructive response than in the event was forthcoming. The ecclesiastical interest in Brandt was as intense as it was surprising. Edward Heath himself addressed over a thousand meetings in the United Kingdom, the majority of them sponsored, supported or attended by Church people. Hardly a significant Church forum did not at some time debate the Brandt Report and the mass lobby of Parliament organised by the World Development Movement in 1981 had Brandt as its centrepiece. After such effort it may seem ungracious to express scepticism about what was achieved. Is it not enough that the Churches tried? Alas no. What matters, surely, is the effect on the poor, on those who are the losers from a system that is clearly exploitative. And that raises the central issue.

For the ecclesiastical enthusiasm for the Brandt Report stems directly from the report's own logic. In conception, it was a brilliant (but specious) attempt to put together a package of proposals that would leave all parties better off – the rich countries (through more stable oil prices); the oil producers (through access to technology and markets); the newly industrialised countries (through a reduction of protectionism) and the poor countries (through an increase in aid). The report was thus a paradigm case of a rationalist solution to the problems of world development, but a rationalist solution set (perhaps oddly in view of the participants) in a political vacuum. By ignoring economic and political conflict within (as well as between) the major groups that it identified, the report was able to pretend that everyone would be better off if only they acted reasonably and sensibly.

While some of the charges from the extreme left – for example that the report was a charter for capitalists – may have been shrill, there can be little doubt that the major philosophical ethos of the report was that of enlightened self-interest which would have most of the structures of the international economy reformed but not reversed. The combination of self-interest and charity proved irresistible to the vast majority of British ecclesiastical opinion.

I don't want to labour the central point, but it is worth giving a slightly different example of the way in which the Churches have found structural issues difficult. They have found them difficult, I argue, both because of their inherent complexity and because of the sociological composition of the Churches themselves. As is now well known that in the period between the two major oil price hikes, that is from 1973 to 1979, many developing countries borrowed heavily from the commercial banks in order to continue to finance their imports. Although the greatest attention has been given to the large Latin American debtors such as Mexico and Argentina, even some of the poorest countries in Africa were caught in the same trap. This is because their debts were denominated in dollars and the rate of interest was floating, that is, it was determined by the domestic rates of interest in the United States.

As the value of the dollar rose against the currencies of the debtor countries; and as interest rates rose in the United States in response to the US deficit; and as the value of the debtor countries' reports declined (even in non-dollar terms); so these countries found themselves in a situation in which it was simply inconceivable that they could repay their debts on schedule. It became almost inconceivable that they could repay them at all. Some countries, for example, were in a position where over half their export earnings were required to service their overseas debts. The effect on the domestic economy of the implied pre-emption of foreign exchange resources is better imagined than described.[14]

The mirror image of that, however, was the fact that the decision by the developing world to borrow from the Western commercial banks had protected tens of thousands – on one estimate, over a million – jobs in the rich world. Here again we see a structural relationship which had the effect of impoverishing the poor while bringing considerable benefit to the rich.

It might be thought that given Old Testament teaching on debt, and the long tradition of the Church's hostility to usury, Western Christendom might have seen the debt issue as one on which the Churches might properly make a contribution. Again it is important to get the nuance right. Certainly there were Church groups in most rich countries calling upon the political leaders to moderate the impact of the debt crisis on the poor countries. Proposals varied from rescheduling debt repayments to cancelling debts owed by the poorest countries. Such proposals, however, came from the specialist development lobby, such as Bread for the World in the United States or the World Development Movement in the United Kingdom; they never became issues around which the proclamation of Kingdom values could take place. Yet here was a nest of issues that, perhaps more than any other, cried out for exposure to the loving generosity, the gratuity, which the Kingdom is supposed to be about.

It is not difficult, however, to see why that didn't happen. When a few tremulous voices did suggest that the Kingdom is about release of debtors from bondage, an outcry went up. A Christian economist, for example, made just such a suggestion in a BBC religious magazine programme at a time when the whole debt crisis was being picked up by the media (late in 1982). The speaker and the BBC were swamped by angry telephone calls and letters from people – some Christians, some not – who saw the security of their bank deposits or the value of their investment in bank shares threatened by any suggestion that loans by banks could be called into question by Biblical authority. This is not to prejudice a difficult and delicate area; a proper analysis of the ethics of the Kingdom and international debt crisis would take a book in itself. I find revealing and apposite, however, the fury and volume of the reaction to the fairly banal suggestion that Christians need to look at the pattern of bank lending from the perspective of the biblical revelation about the nature of God and the nature of humanity. It is revealing in the sense that it demonstrates a cautiousness – to put it mildly – when it is clear that structural change has direct costly consequences for the rich countries. The contrast with the Brandt Report is thus significant. It is apposite in that it demonstrates a failure to take structural issues with a seriousness that is commensurate with their impact on the poor in general, and the poorest people in the poorest countries in particular.

In summary, then, I have argued in this chapter that the Western Churches have failed to come to terms with the structural analysis of poverty at many levels – intellectual, ethical, political and existential. I have been at pains to point out that there have always been voices trying to raise structural issues, but they have been put on the fringes of the debate and have never been 'owned' by the main-line Churches nor by their development agencies. This consistent pattern of marginalisation stems directly from the fact that the Churches themselves are the captives of their own sociological composition and self-understanding. This has meant that even when there is an obvious and direct connection between biblical teaching and the structural analysis of international poverty, the Church is literally incapable of making those connections. We come back again to both historical and sociological inevitability.

Chapter 6

1 Justice and Vision

In the last chapter we saw how structuralist thinking raised issues of justice in and for the Churches by identifying processes that, it claimed, maintained inequality and absolute poverty. In this chapter, we shall first look a little closer at notions of justice as they came to apply to two particular groups which have been denied justice – blacks and women. This will introduce a discussion of the structural position of the poor. In the next chapter we shall examine a particular approach to correcting the injustices suffered by these – and other – groups and see how the Churches were able to respond to that approach.

It is as well to recognise a difficulty at the outset. Racism and sexism, that is the denial of justice to blacks and women, are issues that have an immediacy in the rich countries in a way that mass absolute poverty – the denial of justice to the poor – does not. In the US, the UK, France and, in a slightly different way, Germany, race has become a live social and political issue, and one made the more clamant by the disproportionate effect economic recession has had on blacks and 'guest-workers'. In the same way, sexism has become a political issue with legislation designed to protect women from some of its effects to be found on the statute book in nearly all rich countries. I do not doubt that there is much further to go on both issues, but the point I wish to make is rather different.

Precisely *because* these issues are immediate, existential and often conflictive, they tended to become seen as having a higher priority in the agenda of the Churches than justice for the poor. Even though the issues are much more closely linked than often appears to be the case, the bureaucratic and political procedures of the Churches ensured that race and sex were given a hearing in a way that the structural roots of poverty was not. I am not convinced that, in general, this was a deliberate policy, a kind of smoke-screen which would conveniently mask the difficult issues we raised in the last chapter. To argue that, in the absence of compelling evidence, would be over cynical. More probably, the presence of able and angry spokespeople of blacks and women obliged the Churches to make room for their agendas, at the expense of the agenda of the poor and powerless who, almost by definition, had no such direct representatives in the councils of the Churches at any level, from the international to the local.[1] Let me give a concrete example.

In 1970 the National Council of Churches of the United States, together with the Roman Catholic Episcopal Conference, was on the point of agreeing a major new strategy both to educate American Christians about development and to launch joint action designed to promote development. Riots in Watts and Harlem, and the associated rise of black power, brought to the top of the agenda of both Churches new initiatives, new opportunities, new demands. More particularly, both bureaucracies realised that black people had to be given greater power, had to be listened to more attentively.

Not surprisingly, the item on the top of the agenda of the blacks who managed to establish a toe-hold in the ecclesiastical bureaucracies and hierarchies was the righting of the grievances of their own people. Those grievances went so deep, so close to the heart of the values incarnated in the American Churches, that their correction posed a very deep threat. This challenge to the orthodox structures of the American Churches was so severe that any notion that the American Churches should, or for that matter could, co-operate in the area of international development was simply abandoned.

True, the end of the Vietnam War and the disenchantment with any overseas dimension that overtook American society for ten years played a part. The key factor, however, was the realisation that justice issues at home were so threatening that they had to be digested and institutionalised before any wider work could be attempted.

By the mid-1980s, this process went into reverse. The reassessment by the Churches of the position of the black community both in the Church and in the wider society and, associated with that, the emergence of a less patient, less cautious, less compromising leadership (particularly black leadership) made the American Churches in the National Council of Christian Churches take stronger positions on South African apartheid than at any time in the past. What had been dismissed ten years earlier as a lunatic fringe calling for the withdrawal of Church funds from companies investing in South Africa had, by 1983, become almost an establishment position. The language of justice turns out to have no convenient boundaries.

Or so one would like to think. The experience of the UK in this area is much more ambiguous. The celebrated 'race grants' made by the World Council of Churches to African Nationalist groups in 1972 produced a reaction in many fora of the British Churches that was indistinguishable from rank racism. However clumsily the World Council of Churches may have handled the public relations side of the grants, the fury with which the council was subsequently assailed was a symptom of a national and ecclesiastical pathology which had its roots in the colonial experience.

Many British Christians found it impossible to distinguish between the Church-related development agencies and the World Council of Churches. They expressed their outrage at the latter by withdrawing their support from the former. The smear of 'guns for guerillas', assiduously spread by the New Right, stuck so effectively that the British Church development agencies – and, scarcely less, their American counterparts – simply ignored for twelve crucial years the relationship between racism and poverty.

If the British Churches have largely – and there are many small but striking counter-examples – failed to detect the justice issues at the heart of institutionalised racism, it is not surprising that they have failed to see the justice dimension of the various structural problems that we reviewed in the last chapter. Nor is it surprising that the relationship between justice for non-whites and justice for the poor has been so underappreciated that one has been allowed to be seen as in competition with the other. Indeed, it is arguable that by offering Christians a costless (nearly) salve to their consciences, the Church development agencies have actually delayed the day when the issue of racism has to be faced. For the truth is that people can be persuaded to feel compassionate towards (or, more likely, guilty about) the poor (black or brown) 'out there', while cordially hating the black next door.

For ease of exposition I have, no doubt, overdrawn the contrast between the US where 'the race issue' occluded, for a time, the international poverty issue; and the UK where the latter has often served as a substitute for a serious address to the former. In both countries there are elements of each process. What has been generally lacking is both analysis and action that adequately reflects the mutual interpretation and interdependence of racism and international economic domination. I shall have more to say on this, albeit from a different perspective, in the last two chapters.

2 Justice and Sex

A passion for justice comes from the experience of injustice. Few of us have experienced injustice in the way that black South Africans or Chicano immigrants in the United States, or Turkish workers in Germany, or Indonesians in Holland, or Afro-Caribbean peoples in Brixton or Toxteth have experienced injustice. Yet there is one group of which that is less true – namely women. Led by the remarkable Scarlett Epstein, the 1970s saw an explosion in the professional literature on women in development. Although some of this early literature (Epstein's excluded) was polemical, the basic points it was making were important – and central to a justice agenda.[2] These studies showed that in most developing countries, women in general, and rural women in particular, have been the *victims* of development. Their workload has increased; the absence of their menfolk has increased; their control over family resources has diminished; the volume of those resources itself may have diminished, and the delivery system of the benefits promised by development – education, health, credit – has been systematically biased against them. One has only to look at the proportion of females entering secondary school in relation to the proportion of boys entering secondary school in most African countries to get a flavour of what has been going on. Even in the mid-1980s, three boys go to primary school for every two girls in the thirty-six poorest countries.[3]

Many of the developing agencies had, by the early 1980s, picked up the programmatic implications of this new line of thinking. Many agencies on both sides of the Atlantic began to look much more carefully at the gender of project beneficiaries, and to eliminate so far as possible biases within the design of the project that made it hard for women to participate or get a fair share of the benefits. Projects were designed for women; some were even designed and implemented by women.

Most of the rich country agencies have, then, moved significantly on this issue but find themselves caught in an enfilade. On the one hand their domestic Church base remains substantially sexist at many levels. Consider, for example, the *nature* of the discussions about women's ordination and (in Churches where women are ordained) the promotion of women to significant leadership roles in the Churches in virtually every rich country. That is one side of the crossfire. The other side is the no less – indeed usually rather more – sexist structures of both the Church and the society in which these projects are set. The exploitation of women in India, Africa, or Latin America does not stop because a few British and American social scientists start writing about it.

That this raises some extremely delicate issues need hardly be emphasised. What seems an issue of justice to radical feminists in the United States of America does not necessarily seem an issue of justice to an African bishop in Uganda. Yet the Christian Gospel has traditionally (but possibly mistakenly) been thought to offer universal prescriptions, not on every jot and tittle of social policy but surely on something as fundamental as the exploitation of one half of the human race by the other.

The parallels with racism are uncomfortably close. If racism is abhorrent to the Gospel and everything possible must be done to persuade racists to change their way of looking at the world – and their black neighbour – is it not the case that everything possible must be done to persuade African or Latin American men to change their way of looking at the world – and their women? And yet is this not precisely the crypto-imperialism so vigorously denounced by both far left and far right in the Churches and in society at large? What right have American feminists to tell Third World men to look again at the way they divide the household labour or the household income? While it may be relatively easy to develop a theology of race from Pauline theology of the Church and of redemption, it is a much more sophisticated enterprise to develop a theology of women from New Testament sources in a society in which the beginnings of the change of consciousness about sex roles has yet to emerge.

The two leading justice issues of the mid-1970s to early 1980s in the Churches of the rich North thus presented very different challenges to the whole development enterprise. And yet, as I emphasised in the last paragraph, a critical analysis of the two issues shows them to be surprisingly close. Both struck at assumptions, world views, ways of doing things in the Churches of the rich North at a depth that was, for many Christians, almost unbearably painful. The pathological and neurotic reactions, more evident in the feminist debates than in the race debates (but certainly not absent from the latter), are evidence of just how deep the challenge was going.

Perhaps paradoxically it was easier to cope with that challenge in the case of race, particularly race 'out there', than in the case of sexism/feminism. As charismatic figures like Desmond Tutu and Allan Boesak made a tentative advance less painful than it might otherwise have been, and as repeated violence flared in the townships, it became respectable in most Church circles to express disquiet about what was going on in South Africa and to wonder aloud whether disinvestment, sanctions and the rupture of diplomatic relations were not steps required by the Gospel. By contrast, on feminism, the role of women in the (rich) Church became the dominant question and it was hard to relate that to the wider questions of development, international economic justice and human rights. If the racism issue had the effect of making the Church in the north marginally more aware of racial discrimination in the developing world – and in this limited sense was consciousness-enlarging – the feminist debate in the Churches had the effect of making the Churches more inward looking, more parochial, more defensive. One need only look, for example, at the theological curricula of the leading theological schools and colleges in the United States and in Britain.

I do not wish to deny the importance of validity of much that the feminist theologians are saying: I merely want to point out that just as the initial burst of awareness of the race issue in the

American Churches in the early 1970s hijacked the development debate for ten years, so the current burst of interest in feminism, and all that that implies for patterns of ministry and relationships, has hijacked the development debate in the 1980s. Even though the intellectual groundwork has been done and some (certainly limited and often rather dubious) programmatic experience is available, the debate about the exploitation of women remains, for most Church people in the rich North, to be seen in a much wider context.

3 Justice, Race and Sex; the Language of Power

If race and feminism have been the issues around which the language of justice has forced itself most insistently upon the agenda of the Churches in the rich North, are there analogous issues that have raised the same questions in the Churches in the poor South? There are, of course, *directly* analogous questions, as the Tamil disturbances in Sri Lanka, the Miskito issue in Nicaragua, and the genocide of the indigenous Indian population in Guatemala all tragically attest. The feminist issue has not left the Churches in the developing world wholly untouched either.

The impetus comes not only from expatriate nuns, many of whom are as ready to ask questions about the nature of authority in a male-dominated Church in the mission field as they are in their country of origin. There is a more home-grown reassessment of the role of women in progress, though sometimes it takes surprising forms. I remember visiting a wholly indigenous Church training centre in Namibia. I was courteously conducted round the various departments – youth, mission, service, women's work, music, biblical studies. The tour ended at the imposing Church, right at the centre of the extensive compound. I was taken aback to find pinned on the Church door a large poster depicting Mrs Thatcher in all her post-Falklands euphoria. I asked my guides why it was there. I was met with many charming African evasions: courteous, amusing, but determinedly opaque.

Over the subsequent meal I became better acquainted with some of the women working at the centre and, recollecting myself, managed to conduct the conversation in the indirect parabolic way in which serious conversation is politely conducted in many African circles. Eventually the truth came out. 'We needed to tell the men,' said one of the particularly impressive women, 'that it's time they recognised that leaders do not necessarily have to be men. If Mrs Thatcher can win a war for Britain, maybe women can win a battle or two for the Kingdom of God.'

For the purposes of this argument I do not wish, however, to explore these parallel issues, not because they are not directly relevant to development, nor least of all because they are unimportant in themselves. Instead, I want to take the analysis a step further. I want to suggest that the issues of race and feminism are essentially about power. The race issue is at bottom a question about the power of the dominant race over the dominated race. What gives feminism its edge is that women feel dominated by men in an asymmetrical power relationship.

This takes us to the heart of the most difficult part of the Churches' role in development. The issue can be put simply, if still crudely, like this; a key component of development (indeed, of the process of becoming fully human) is, so some people have argued, the process by which poor people cease to be the object of blind forces and / or of other people's wills. To take control of one's own destiny and accept responsibility for one's life and the choices it poses is central both to personal and societal development. It is central both to the inward journey of inner transformation and the outward journey of structural change that makes justice possible.

This process of taking control of one's destiny is essentially (that is, in essence) a matter of taking power. It is a matter of taking power over one's own inner demons and sources of corruption, through allowing the redeeming grace of God to work at the deepest levels of one's psyche. But it is also a question of taking power to confront the people, the institutions and the relationships that seek to use one as an object to be disposed of, as a pawn in their own game. The persons thus confronted may be landowners, or money lenders or employers or bureaucrats, or politicians or corrupt judges; and the institutions may be co-operatives or credit societies or political parties or even families.

4 The Net and the Magnet

An illustration will help clarify the processes at work. First I will describe the social processes, basing the description on a detailed study of certain villages in Bangladesh undertaken by the Bangladesh Rural Advancement Committee and entitled, revealingly, *The Net*.[4] The researchers found that the great majority of goods and services designed for the benefit of the poor were, in fact, being appropriated by non-poor operators. They were then either consumed directly or redistributed to favoured clients of those operators in exchange for specified services – labour, votes, silence.

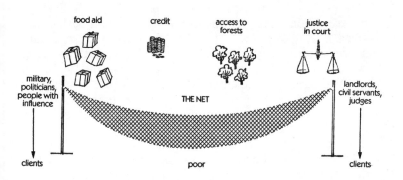

As the diagram indicates, the range of goods and services involved is substantial, perhaps even comprehensive, from food aid supplied by overseas donors (either official or non-governmental) to a fair hearing in court from a magistrate who has not been bribed or intimidated. Because all of these benefits have to pass through the hands of administrators of one kind or another – from forest rangers who grant permits to scavenge firewood, to civil servants who run feeding programmes (or grant permission to foreign agencies to run such programmes) – the possibilities for appropriating a large, sometimes the entire, part of the benefits for reassignment to clients are clearly enormous.

Two questions then become important. Who are these clients? And what proportion of the benefits do they in fact acquire? In general, the clients are those who can perform a service for the patron; it is usually (though not universally) a reciprocal relationship. Small services attract small benefits; significant services, especially those associated with land disputes (e.g. favourable testimony in court), bring larger rewards. Sometimes, then, the people offering these services will indeed be poor; they will be the intended beneficiaries, but to become so they will have been obliged to collude in the process of strengthening the economic and/or political position (and typically the two go hand in hand) of the non-poor.

That helps us answer the second question. It is hard to generalise about the proportion of the benefits that are hijacked by the non-poor. The BRAC study suggests a very high proportion indeed, but that could be an extreme case. What is clear, however, is that the *process* has the long-term effect of entrenching and enlarging the control of the non-poor over the poor. The system will therefore tend towards a situation in which more and more 'external' benefits are used by the non-poor for their own advantage.

Someone may say: 'That's too simple. For the real struggle is not between the poor and the non-poor. It is between different factions within the non-poor; and if the poor got their act together, they could play one faction off against the other and capture more of the benefits. The poor are poor because they are dumb or lazy.'

In theory that is a reasonable argument. In practice, as anyone who has lived in the rural areas of the Indian sub-continent (and, increasingly, Africa) knows too well, rural politics are not run according to reasonable argument. Violence, intimidation, force are the hallmarks of rural politics in these areas as much as they are the hallmarks of national politics in Central Africa. If the poor try to duck the system, to manipulate the manipulators, they discover very quickly where real power lies.

What is to be done? Notice that on this account the poor are not poor because they are genetically or personally inferior.

Nor are they the victims of a culture of poverty out of which they are unable and/or unwilling to escape.[5] They are poor because other groups, other classes in at least some senses of that term, have interests that are in conflict with their interests – and enough power over them to ensure that their interests take precedence. Notice, too, how broadly based is that superior power. It is not just that they have more money or political influence. Certainly they have that; but they also have literacy, access to information, access to networks of influence, mobility and spare resources (so that they can take risks and/or a longer view of things).

Given these huge asymmetries of power, we can extend BRAC's analysis a step further and argue that it is not only the case that these powerful groups prevent external resources reaching the poor – in significant quantities or at all. They are also able to appropriate whatever wealth the poor have. The net is also a magnet.

The most widely researched field in which this can be shown to happen is in access to land, almost the key to life itself in countries where wage-employment in the rural areas is scarce, seasonal and poorly-paid. The poorer families often share-crop some land: the poorest cultivators will *only* share-crop, having no land of their own. Access to land therefore depends on landowners being willing to make land available for renting in this way. It is clear, however, that the advent of the so-called Green Revolution, based on high-yielding seed varieties and fertilisers, changed the interests of the landowners. It was now in their interest to farm the land themselves, partly because of economies of scale and partly because it was, especially in the early stages of the Green Revolution, more profitable to do so. Land was therefore taken away from share-croppers. If they had no land of their own, they became landless labourers, competing in an over-supplied market for work. The magnet had sucked away their one access to a more or less secure livelihood.[6]

It is immediately obvious that, if this account of the nature of rural society is at all accurate – and I believe it is, at least in general terms – the naive/optimistic and modernising approach to development, based on scattered projects is, at best, likely to benefit the non-poor more than the poor. For unless the project can transform rural power relations, the benefits will, almost inexorably, slide back to the landowners, money-lenders, administrators and politicians. The question then becomes a stark but difficult one; is there any way in which people from 'outside' (and 'outside' starts three miles down the road) can change the distribution of power within the village?

5 Power, Development and the Church

It is hard to exaggerate the scale and complexity of that task. Before turning, in the next chapter, to consider how it has been tackled, three introductory comments are worth making. First, I have posed the question in terms of rural Bangladesh or India. Arguably the exploitative nature of rural power relations are most stark there, not least because land is short and differences of class and/or caste are deeply embedded in social and psychological structures. We should not make the mistake, however, of assuming that the processes I have described are unique to the Indian sub-continent. Studies of *ujamaa* villages in Tanzania, co-operatives in Kenya, of the operations of market mammies in Ghana, of landowners in Egypt, tell the same story in a different key.

Nor is this essentially a rural phenomenon. The relationships become more complicated and sometimes more abstract when one moves to an urban setting, but the relations between a sweat-shop owner and his employees are not *that* different to the relations between a landlord and a share-crop tenant.[7] Interests diverge and are seen (rightly or wrongly) as a zero sum game – more for me means less for you. And power is asymmetrical: he can fire me, I cannot fire him.

This raises the second point. It is but a short step from the realities of the last paragraph to questions about the nature of economic organisation. Or, to put it bluntly, is the problem inherent in capitalism, so that an assault on the distribution of power is actually an assault on capitalism? And if that is the case, does it not follow that the more direct approach is to work for the overthrow of capitalism, rather than tamper with one of its pathological symptoms? It will be no surprise to hear that different groups answer such a question in different ways. Some Marxists, for example, point out that capitalism proper is not yet fully established in most parts of the developing world, and that it is futile to try to overthrow it until its inner contradictions themselves render it unviable. At the other end of the ideological spectrum, it is argued that in so far as inequitable distribution of power is a direct consequence of capitalism (rather than a quite separate phenomenon stemming from deep cultural roots), it can be tackled by law and proper judicial arrangements. For the essence of law, of justice, is that it protects the weak from the strong. What is required, then, is a properly functioning, independent judiciary and clearly codified law that has the essential nature of justice at its heart. People in the middle of the ideological spectrum might well wonder how that can be achieved in practice, when law and its administration are so evidently part of the outworkings of the inequitable distribution of power. We shall have to return to this debate in a slightly different mode.

Third introductory point: Christians usually find notions of power extremely difficult. This phenomenon takes a number of forms: from an exaggerated reluctance to take politics seriously, to a no less exaggerated projection of powerlessness as the defining characteristic of Jesus's personality. Walter Wink, whose path-breaking work we shall have to return to later, has commented on the almost wilful misreading of the biblical record by generations of scholars and lay people, who have failed to see that power is a central biblical concept and the questions it raises – of its origins, its use and abuse – are a central biblical concern.[8] Compared with Wink's detailed analysis of biblical power-language, traditional Christian coyness about power seems odd to the point of pathological. Perhaps at some deep, sub-conscious level, we fear that if we face the radical questions about power which the Bible poses we shall find ourselves and our own structural position too fundamentally threatened.

If we take these three comments together – the universality of questions of power in the process of development; the possible relationship between power and economic organisation; and the depth of traditional Christian resistance to the analysis of power relations – we see that Christians who want to enable poor people to design their own authentic pattern of development are likely to run into three critical areas. First, they have to find a method whereby the poor can change the

Chapter 7

In the last chapter we saw that justice issues are reducible to power issues. If there is no genuinely independent legislature and judiciary to ensure the rights of the poor and powerless are respected, those rights have to be asserted by the poor themselves acquiring sufficient countervailing power.

The operational question then becomes one of method. How can poor people be enabled to assert their rights, against, for example, the operators of the net? It is fair to say that this is not a new question. Some, like Oscar Lewis and the Culture of Poverty school, have declared it to be unanswerable in those terms. Others, many missionaries among them, thought that the answer lay in education of a more or less traditional variety. Evangelicals thought the process of conversion itself would overcome the lethargy and fatalism they believed they observed among the heathen villages of India and Africa. It was, however, Paulo Freire, a Brazilian Roman Catholic teacher and educational theorist, who produced, in 1972, the book that was to prove a milestone in this debate.[1]

Freire had spent much of his life in North-East Brazil and had seen, in that deeply polarised society, the psychological as well as the social effects of extreme poverty and the unequal distribution of power. For Freire there could be no enduring approach to the former without a solution to the latter. As long as peasants were caught in a web of exploitative and oppressive relationships with the money-lender, the store-keeper, the landowner, the merchant, the truck operator and the police, the combined operations of the net and the magnet would ensure that poverty could at best be relieved – it could never be eliminated.

Freire argued that peasants were not 'simple' or 'primitive', even though the vast majority of them were illiterate. They were perfectly capable of thinking things through, but lacked a critical awareness of their own position in the scheme of things. Often they were conscious that the price in the local store was double that in the stores in town; or that the police had to be bribed; or that the landowner was holding land he neither used nor allowed others to use. These were taken as facts of life, undifferentiated from the fact that the sun rises in the east or that the rains sometimes fail (one, notice, predictable and regular; the other unpredictable, irregular but not infrequent).

What was lacking in this view of the world, Freire argued, was first the need for an explanatory frame, i.e. a realisation that the fact that the landowner will not let me graze my goat on his unused pasture *needs* explaining. And, second, the confidence to look for, find and act on that explanation.

Together these constituted what Freire called critical awareness or, unbeautifully, conscientisation. It was *critical* in that it looked for explanations and subjected those explanations to ethical critique: was it right that he put up my rent when he already had great wealth and my child is malnourished? It was *awareness* because it invited the participants to a deeper knowledge of their whole environment, particularly their relational environment, a knowledge, moreover, that was not only dispassionate intellectual knowledge (knowledge *about*), but affective, feeling knowledge (knowledge *of*).

It is not necessary in a book as short as this to go into the details either of Freire's underlying educational philosophy or of his method. The key point of the former is, however, important. It can be summed up like this: the purpose of education is to allow people to become subjects rather than objects, to control their own destinies rather than be the victims of the desires or social processes of others. The philosophical and psychological origins of such a view are clear enough, and perhaps already look dated: the duality subject/object is obviously (now) too simplistic, too overdrawn. To be fair, Freire sometimes recognised that, but in the hands of less scholarly disciples and practitioners his own qualifications were quickly lost. Nonetheless, the political and programmatic implications are dynamite, for they mean that the end of education becomes a total change in the way individuals and groups relate to and deal with each other. Revolution is hardly too strong a word. Shorn of its romantic, First Empire connotations, it is an accurate one.

Little need be said of Freire's method because it has been adapted and revised to fit local situations the world over.[2] Freire himself used literacy classes as a way of raising critical consciousness. This had the advantage of creating a group with its own peer loyalties and a commitment to some kind of self-improvement from the start. The emphasis on the group is central for Freire. Because he sees the poor as victims of *social* pressures and relationship, his own commitment is to social change rather than individual advancement. Furthermore, the group develops its own learning/teaching dynamic, so that members teach each other and enlarge the consciousness of the whole group through that process.

Freire's followers soon discovered that literacy work was not the only outer process within which the inner task of discovering a critical awareness could be implanted. Specifically, parish priests and catechists who were attracted by Freire's analysis and method soon found that Christian teaching and preaching could be readily adapted.[3] The teaching process thus ceased to be an externally imposed corpus of facts and ethics about an alien culture, and became a process of reflection about a community's own life, its constraints and determinants. Ernesto Cardenal has left us a fine example of this process at work. Here is an extract from a discussion on the second temptation (Luke 4:5–7), among the peasants of Solentiname, in Nicaragua in the early 1970s.[4]

Laureano: 'He's like a politician, that devil. Because that's what political campaigns are like. A man comes into a town and makes all kinds of promises so people will vote for him. And people do vote for him and afterwards he doesn't give them shit.'

Another says: 'The devil wanted Jesus to adore him so he could be God.'

And another: 'He was offering him an imperialist messianism.'

'Then imperialism would be all right if it was the imperialism of Jesus?' asked Julio.

Felipe: 'No, because if Jesus had fallen into temptation his imperialism would have been just like the others'.'

Tomás: 'Just like theirs, because they're under the power of the devil.'

Tono: 'There's one thing here: The devil is making him a false proposal. He tells Jesus that he's going to give him all the power and the riches of the world, and Jesus, by refusing, is stating that the true master is himself, that is, all of humanity. And he doesn't have to adore the devil to get him to give Jesus what is rightly his. And that's our situation, too.'

I said: 'Why do you suppose the devil says that he has received all this?'

William: 'He grabbed it all. It's a dictatorship. He has the power, but a power that is not legitimate. It's stolen. Imperialism and capitalism and all oppression belong to him...'

It is, of course, one thing to enable the poor and the powerless to appreciate the reality of their own structural situation – that politicians let them down, that illegitimate power is used against them, that there is a devilish quality about inequality and inequity. It is quite another to know how to harness the energy thus released at two levels – the outer level of action and the inward level of psychological and spiritual adjustment. At its least creative, this energy can spark unproductive or even counterproductive overt opposition to the abuses of power by the ruling groups. Inwardly it can produce such levels of anger, frustration and resentment that it becomes exceedingly hard to use the new level of consciousness creatively.

Freire was never under any illusion but that conscientisation would indeed lead to conflict. His educational purpose was to change the distribution of power. That is seldom achieved without conflict: indeed a conflict-free exchange of power is unlikely to be effective since it is in the process of the struggle for power that the powerless become first to wield it. Freire, however, hoped that non-violent resistance would achieve the redistribution of power required. In this he followed in the tradition of Gandhi, though he, unlike Gandhi, never worked out a methodology of non-violent resistance to accompany the process of conscientisation. He seems to have thought, at least when he wrote *The Pedagogy of the Oppressed*, that the creation of alternative centres of power in society – e.g. effective peasants' organisations – would lead to a process of negotiation and a new deal for the poor. In such a hope he perhaps allowed his own gentle spirit to triumph over the realities of rural politics in most parts of the world.

For the facts surely are that *effective* organisations of *critically aware* peasants are a source of great threat to rural élites and their clients since they threaten the whole apparatus of the net. They must therefore be contained, resisted or destroyed. I will illustrate that reaction shortly.

It is no surprise, perhaps, to find that Freire's ideas found a ready audience among younger Latin American theologians trying to articulate an account of the faith that did justice to the context in which most of the faithful live in Latin America – a context of fear, deprivation and oppression. The whole motif of liberation theology, with its heavy emphasis on social analysis, on the validity of experience of the poor, on a radical break from the past of bondage and on the hope of a more glorious future, that whole motif was not only consistent with Freire's pedagogy, it also underpinned it and was itself underpinned by it.

Liberation theology in the hands of Guittierez, Miranda and, in a slightly different form, Boff, thus became a religious language in which the elements of Freire's method were encoded. To many people both in Latin America and the rich Churches, the liberation theologians were announcing that conscientisation confrontation and even class struggle were not only necessary parts of 'development'; they were necessary parts of the living out of the Gospel in the social contexts I have described.

It was this conjunction of a deeply worked out theory of conscientisation and an evolving theology of liberation which proved so powerful a set of ideas, especially but by no means exclusively, in Latin America. Together they shifted the language and substance of the Church's role in development. For those who had read Freire and Guittierez, 'development' became a term of abuse, almost on a par with 'gringo'. Development became associated with modernisation, reformism, gradualism; with the continuing domination of US multinationals, US culture and US military might; with the insidious and irreversible effects of capitalism and its class structures. I remember giving a lecture at the Jesuit University in Manila in 1970. I had run through contemporary economic theories of development when I was interrupted by an angry student at the back of the hall. 'Are you for development or for liberation?' he demanded. So starkly was the dichotomy seen. 'Development' might be a concern of the West, the Western Churches and their aid agencies. To these young Jesuits and their students, spending time as many of them did in the shocking slums of Metro Manila, the key questions were quite different. They were about what would free poor people from the forces that held them captive. The language of Exodus had acquired a new relevance – and a new urgency.

It is time now, therefore, to reflect on the challenge the Freire approach posed to the development work of the Churches. (In this connection it is not irrelevant to note in passing that Freire worked at, or in close association with, the World Council of Churches from 1970–72.) Note first and most obviously what a contrast lies between the traditional top-down, modernising, neatly planned project so beloved of donors and a programme of conscientisation. The latter is a process that is not reducible to a project. It cannot be timetabled or planned in the tidy way demanded by project-dominated donors. It is simply not open to the managerial manipulations of Western categories of thought. It has to be organic, inevitably slow, uncertain, unpredictable, in many senses uncontrollable. Because it is essentially about freeing people in a number of dimensions simultaneously, a process dealing with dimensions of life that are complex, inter-active and hard to get at, it is an approach that has to be lived experimentally, experientially and always provisionally. It is therefore an approach that is always opaque and untidy for those outside it. From that it follows that it is hard for the external donor (external, that is, to the process itself whether they be nationals or expatriates) to relate to the process in a way that is genuinely supportive. Even more than in the case of projects, external relationships can easily be rendered destructive or subversive or diversionary. I can best illustrate how disastrous that can be from my own sad, and perhaps even bitter, experience.

When this whole approach was still in its very early days, I was sent by an ecumenical agency to help establish a centre in Bolivia where peasants could be enabled to set up their own associations through the application of this kind of methodology. We worked hard to secure land, minimal buildings and key personnel. The classes began initially, as in the classic

Freire methodology, with literacy. Reasonably satisfied that my work in establishing the centre was finished I returned to Europe. A month later, a posse of local land owners had burnt the centre to the ground and shot the leader. Of course, I should have foreseen this possibility and gone about the whole process in a way that was less visible, less 'projectified', depending more on the skill, wisdom and innate leadership of the peasants themselves. My stupidity, and the whole environment out of which I came and in which the agency I was working for was set, had combined to produce a tragic self-defeating outcome.

Second, we have already seen that the development agencies need – or feel they need – 'successes' with which to reassure or encourage their supporters, yet conscientisation-type pro-grammes tend to produce little that can legitimately be described as 'success' in the terms required by the agencies. Indeed, that whole way of thinking falls back into the language and thought forms of the modernisation paradigm, which are inappropriate to this approach.

If one searches for 'success', one can identify particular areas or particular groups which have literally changed beyond recognition as a result of the application of this method. I can think of groups of peasants in the Philippines, in Sri Lanka, in Nigeria and in Nicaragua whose lives have been literally transformed by the inward and outward journeys from object to subject that is implied in the Freire method.

Take, for example, a group of peasants on the northern frontier of Nicaragua constantly harassed by attacks from the so-called Contras. They are not the passive dupes of a communist-leaning government that right-wing propaganda in America and in Europe makes them out to be. Indeed, one of the heartening aspects of this process is how ready it has made the peasants to challenge and confront the party leadership of the Sandinistas. On a number of issues – from conscientious objection to the provision of transport – they have confronted the local party secretary, who freely admits that he has had to modify policies as a result of pressure from this group of peasants.

At the same time, the peasants' living standards have risen dramatically by comparison with the period under Somoza. It is, of course, a matter of judgment as to how far this change in living standards is attributed to changes in agricultural policy.[5] Well-informed local observers, however, were clear that the peasants could never have run their own cooperative as well as they were now doing if they had not been through the experience of the Freire method. To that extent, changes in agricultural policy may have been a necessary condition of the improvement of their way of life: they were not, according to these observers, a sufficient condition. That raises a very important issue to which we shall have to return, but for the moment we need to ask how the local Churches have responded to the bush fire of the Freire method, as it has spread throughout the developing world.

It will come as no surprise to discover that there is no common picture. As soon as one looks beyond the rhetoric of Councils of Churches or Bishops' Conferences or synods and actually enquires what is happening on the ground, very substantial differences appear even within the same Church or denomination in the same country. Indeed, I have come across one Central American diocese of the Roman Catholic Church where the bishop was a colonel in the army and some of his priests were in the forefront of enabling the peasants to adopt the approach I have described! The bishop stood for a very traditional type of development, with the army playing both a modernising and a repressive role; the clergy stood for a totally different approach in which it was hoped, in the longer term at least, the peasants would control more and more of the means of production and slowly erode the power base of the local oligarchs, many of them military men.

It has proved impossible to discern any tidy, clear-cut pattern. For example, I started with the working hypothesis that local churches or Church development agencies which were heavily dependent on project-oriented, overseas donors would be most resistant to the Freire methods. One can certainly find evidence of this connection. In many development agencies, in poor countries, there exists a tension between the need to generate projects to secure overseas finance (and not unimportantly, pay the overheads of the agency concerned) and the growing conviction that without the empowerment of the peasants in both the senses I have described, such projects are likely to prove illusory – with the benefits caught by the net or attracted by the magnet.

Equally there are emerging slowly, inadequately and often reluctantly, Church-related donors in the rich North who are prepared to fund the untidy processes of empowerment, at least as long as they can be presented to donors and/or co-financing government agencies as literacy work or community development. It goes without saying that those donor agencies tend to be the ones that are least dependent on government financing, if only because the kind of administrative arrangements and project criteria that governments insist on would make it extremely difficult (without straight falsification) to submit this type of programme for government funding.

It will already be clear that I am reluctant to leap to a generalisation about the relationships between institutional Churches and the Freire method. I am reluctant, partly because there is a huge empirical task here which, so far as I am aware, has not been undertaken. But I am reluctant, too, because the pattern is constantly changing and is, as I have already indicated, extremely complex even at the local level. It is with some misgivings then that I shall venture to make one or two observations which should be interpreted as impressions. Although the style is indicative, the mood is interrogative.

The number of cases in which Church authorities have moved against conscientisation activities is not known, but the stories reporting such moves are too frequent on all three major continents of the developing world to be dismissed lightly. It is very easy to see how this might occur. Here is a not wholly imaginary reconstruction.

A group of hitherto docile, unresponsive peasants (or their urban equivalents) became influenced, and perhaps organised, by a development worker whose contact with, and answerability to, the institutional Church, may have been slender. Peasants, let us say belonging to a particular church congregation begin to stir at a number of psychological and social levels. They start asking questions. They ask questions about themselves; they ask questions about the social environment in which they are placed; they ask questions about the relationship between the Church and, let us say, the local landowner or the local military chief or the local money-lender.

They may not be entirely satisfied with the answers they get. They therefore begin to put questions to their priest and, increasingly confident of their own ability to reflect upon the answers they receive, they challenge the priest. Perhaps used to more traditional forms of authority and relationships with his people, the priest feels deeply threatened by the new relationship that is beginning to emerge. He complains to his bishop. The bishop complains to the Council of Churches, which in turn complains to the agency which is sponsoring the work with the peasants. Give or take a few details, I have seen this happen in Kenya, Zambia, Tanzania, India and Brazil.

Against that experience, however, has to be set the fact that there have been courageous Church leaders who have protected conscientisation programmes from secular and ecclesiastical authorities that see themselves threatened by them. I can think of one senior Roman Catholic bishop in Brazil who was threatened with death by a right wing extremist group, precisely because he refused to close down the conscientisation activities in one part of his diocese. Nonetheless, we need to be aware that the process itself will perhaps inevitably raise questions about the nature, use and abuse of ecclesiastical authority. Some theological and ecclesiastical traditions are better able to cope with that family of questions than others.

The second general observation that has to be made is that it often proves difficult to hold together the two levels of transformation that I have referred to as the inward journey and the outward journey. That should be no surprise: the metropolitan Churches ceased to hold it together centuries ago. Indeed, some people would argue that it hasn't been held together properly since the Constantinian settlement. It is in my experience, however, a feature of the Freire method that people get so engrossed in and excited by the political and social dimension of the method that the inner transformation can sometimes get short shrift or simply be forgotten.

That is a betrayal of Freire's best insights (just as it is a betrayal of the best insights of the liberation theologians who produced a kind of theological counterpoint to Freire's own work). I shall have more to say about this later, but note for the moment that many conservative (in both a political and a theological sense) Church leaders find it difficult to endorse conscientisation programmes which seem to them to be 'no more than' initial steps in political indoctrination. Some clergy become critical of the conscientisation process, not because of its ultimate political manifestations (which, after all, take a long time to appear), but because the first effect of conscientisation is to remove the people involved in the process from public worship and from the everyday activities of the Church. What this implies about 'Church' and Kingdom will occupy us in the last three chapters.

It is not my purpose at this stage to debate the comparative validity of a privatised cult as against materialistic politics: both are so inadequate as to make such a debate uninteresting. I merely record that a good deal of ecclesiastical opposition to conscientisation has arisen from the fact that the inward journey easily gets given too little prominence. The first symptom of this neglect is the gradual alienation of those engaged from the public life of the Church.

Finally, we have to face squarely – perhaps more squarely than Freire himself did – the fact that conscientisation is likely to result in conflict and even violence. That is why, incidentally, Freire has been working on a pedagogy of the rich, because he could see that they needed liberation from the inner drives and outer resistances that are the mirror image of the liberation of the poor and the oppressed. For unless the rich and the powerful are thus liberated from their need to hang on to their wealth and their power in an exclusive and defensive way, the process of conscientisation is likely, if it is successful, to lead ultimately to a confrontation – a confrontation, that is, between the rich and the poor who demand a reorganisation of social processes in a way which will enable them to be less poor and less at the power of others.

This conflict can be ugly. Although some programmes now incorporate a conscious attempt to build into the conscientisation process an appreciation of the power of non-violent resistance or passive protest, it is fair to say that this theme is still relatively undeveloped (as, indeed, it is in the metropolitan Churches).

Christians find conflict very difficult and for the most part Church leaders regard the avoidance of conflict, particularly conflict that might become violent, as one of the first objectives of Church policy. If there is a straight choice – in Latin America and in Asia that is often how it looks at village level – between peace and justice, Church leaders will often opt for peace, conveniently sliding over the extremely demanding conditions for peace that both the Old Testament and New make quite explicit.[6] They ignore too the fact that 'peace' is often experienced by the poor as the very reverse of peace, that is, the endurance of violence.

One further relationship that has been affected by the spread of conscientisation processes is immediately relevant to our purposes. I have already commented on the emergence of the new brand of Church development official in the developing world. Often impatient of the structures in which they find themselves and politically more radical than Church leadership, these development workers find themselves challenged, in a most interesting way, by the processes I have been describing. On the one hand, they understand the theory and have often seen the results of conscientisation on the ground. Furthermore, most of them would endorse the ideological and political stance of conscientisation and see it both pragmatically and theologically as the most effective way the Churches have for work with the poor.

At the same time, many of them find it hard to relate to the process and often feel threatened by it. Nurtured in a modernisation, project-dominated tradition, and constantly under pressure from their own hierarchies and their donor 'partners' to generate discrete, fundable projects with a clearly defined output, these development workers find themselves torn in two. They know they have to play the project game in order to survive institutionally, and even in terms of their own careers, but they know, too, that long-term improvement of the lot of most peasants is going to depend on a process which almost by its very nature is something from which they are excluded.

Different individuals in different structural situations inevitably react in dissimilar ways to the challenges this poses. The tensions this generates are perhaps most obvious in India, where many young development workers, coming from Christian backgrounds or having worked in Church-based organisations, find they can no longer support the kind of project-based development that their institutions and the associated donors are demanding. The best of them go off to the villages to work with the peasants, often putting themselves at great personal risk in the process.

For reasons that are easily understandable, they tend then to overpaint the contrast between the work they are doing, admirable as much of it may be, and the work of the Church-based development groups, which they represent as old-fashioned, ineffective, top-down and heavily bureaucratic. This very attitude, of course, deepens the already existing chasm between the Church development institutions on the one hand, and the work of conscientisation in the villages on the other. It is not unknown for this chasm to be so deep that communication breaks down completely. This results in isolating the Church development agencies from a most important part of their agenda and, as it were, coralling them even tighter into modernising projects and all the ambiguities this involves.

Before we leave this topic we have to ask one central but immensely difficult question: Can conscientisation work, in the sense that it can deliver people from the forces that make them objects and enable them to take responsibility for their own lives? To use slightly more abstract language, is conscientisation a necessary or a sufficient condition of authentic development? Conscientisation has its passionate advocates, its inventive adaptors, its sceptics and its implacable critics. We need to recognise at the start that at least some of this spectrum of reaction is attributable to the fact that people mean different things by the same word and have very different experiences of it in practice. For example, I myself would be extremely critical of some programmes that use the name conscientisation, primarily because I would have to admit that they have become no more than slightly disguised political indoctrination courses. Similarly, I have witnessed the process at work in a way that is clearly and palpably transforming people's lives. We return to problems of definition and the variability of experience.

We also return to a much deeper problem of the relationship between change in personal and group consciousness on the one hand, and the policy and legislative environment in which that consciousness exists on the other. Let me illustrate. A conscientisation programme in South Africa is clearly a very different proposition from a conscientisation programme in Nicaragua or Tanzania. Similarly, a conscientisation programme in Brazil or even Argentina is a different proposition to a similar programme in Chile. In other words, where the government is (however imperfectly and however inadequately) trying to address the issues of the poor and unimportant, the point of conflict with the established powers is likely to be much further down the track than in a country in which the government is allied openly and militarily with the existing forces of oppression. To put it at its simplest, a conscientisation programme in a country in which the government is committed to raising the level of living, broadly defined, of the poorest, is much more likely to be successful than a conscientisation programme in a country in which the government regards the poor and marginal people as either dispensable (as in South Africa) or a threat (as in Guatemala) or as a political variable to be manipulated (as in many states of India).

And yet... and yet... and yet... I feel obliged to say that even in the most repressive situation – and I think of Duvalier's Haiti and Pinochet's Chile – I have come across groups that have a dignity, a self-awareness, a determination, and a courage that may have little to do with development as modernisers or structuralists conceive of it, but which has everything to do with development in terms of personal and community growth. Poor and exploited they may be; supine flotsam at the behest of external pressure they certainly are not.

Finally, there is a deeper point. Conscientisation may mobilise people to confront the net and the magnet. Handled properly, that can be creative and it can ensure that goods and services which are supposed to teach the poor do in fact do so. However the 'subjectification' of poor people that Freire was trying to bring about is unlikely to mean a great deal unless it is accompanied by the control of productive assets. To put it crudely, peasants may be well-organised and motivated to tackle the local power structure: but unless they have land, tools, seeds and markets they will remain poor. Too much of the Church's work in conscientisation, including that of the so-called base communities, has overlooked this fundamental point, often on the assumption that once the local power blocs are confronted, boring questions about production and management will automatically solve themselves.

It is hard to imagine a more wrong-headed and ultimately self-defeating assumption. And this is for two reasons. First, even if the process of confrontation does produce assets (e.g. land as a result of the implementation of a land reform statute), those assets have to be managed properly if they are to be productive. If they are not made productive, the poor are no better off in a physical, material sense: and, secondly, the assets will quickly be reappropriated by the élite and their friends. In other words, it is pointless just to break the net. The assets of the poor have to become sufficiently 'weighty' to defy the magnet – or they will simply be sucked back. Unfortunately, it is often the case that programmes and personnel that are good at enabling peasants to acquire a critical consciousness of their social and political environment are almost useless at securing the material base of the peasants thus conscientised. In my view, such programmes are not only likely to be proved ineffective in the long run: they are also in essence cruel and manipulative.

Chapter 8

To summarise the argument so far, I have suggested that a large number of people in the industrialised countries are readily moved by the observed plight of poor people caught up in the aftermath of man-made or natural disasters. That natural pity forms the continuing backdrop against which the Western Churches became historically – and become existentially – involved in the process of development.

It is important to note both the historical dimension and the existential dimension. By that I mean that we can trace the Churches' thinking and action over time from the late 1950s to the present day and observe a process of change taking place. We can also, however, take a vertical cross-cut through the Churches' present involvement and find different groups, different constituencies at the various levels exposed by that cross-cut.

Perhaps an analogy will make that clearer. If you take a hundred amateur but competent artists, you are likely to find styles that range from creditable copies of Constable through Turner to the Impressionists to Picasso to, let us say, Ben Nicholson. Furthermore, over his own lifetime an artist may change his style from that of prettily representational to deeply symbolic. There are thus three dimensions to be observed. There is the historical dimension, the way dominant schools have changed over time. There is the range of styles currently being adopted. And there is the change over time of the style of any one artist, who may move within his own expression along a part of that historical experience and contribute his own understanding and synthesis of it.

That analogy lets us see why the picture is necessarily confused and complicated. In the foregoing chapters I have tried to sketch out what I perceive as the historical process of the Church's coming to grips with world poverty, but at each point I have been aware that a vertical cross-cut would reveal that, whatever the dominant view, there would be variants, with different groups at different levels of understanding and engagement.

Today, therefore, one can find Christians and groups representing them – as the Ethiopian crisis so amply demonstrated – exclusively concerned with the immediate relief of immediate needs. Simultaneously, one can find groups involved in the modernisation paradigm, perhaps most spectacularly in the improvement of African agriculture. One can also find groups trying to raise some of the structural questions through, for example, financing land reform or co-operatives. And one can find groups engaged in justice issues, in conscientisation and in questions of the distribution and use of power that those raise.

Some of the large Church development agencies both in the metropolitan countries and in the developing world itself may well be engaged in a number of these activities simultaneously. Virtually every Church development agency operates an emergency unit or funds emergency programmes. The vast majority put most of their resources into modernisation activities; relatively few into structural, justice or power-type programmes.

From the perspective of the developing countries themselves, we have seen how the same spectrum, from relief to conscientisation, has developed and how the same co-existence of various types of involvement continue. We saw how conscientisation and its variants have posed a particular difficulty to both the leadership of the main institutional Churches and to the new generation of professional Church development workers nurtured in the project cycle. We have seen too that whereas the modernisation approach is supposedly consensual, the conscientisation approach is inevitably conflictive. We have seen how this poses a number of problems at various levels – pragmatic, ethical, theological, psychological.

I have summarised the argument at this length because I want to draw out an interesting parallel. It is, however, a parallel that isn't quite parallel! Conscientisation has obliged many groups of poor and powerless people and those who work with them to take as central the category of power.

Simultaneously, the justice issues which I illustrated with reference to race and feminism, but which have a much wider application in international economic relations, have put primary emphasis on power. The power of whites has been challenged by blacks. The power of men has been challenged by women. In the international arena, the power of the rich countries to fix the rules of the game in their own favour has been challenged. The realisation of the *centrality of power* is what gives this pattern its parallelism.

We have to be clear, however, that in the first case it is those who are the victims of the abuse of power who are raising the questions: in the second case that does not, and perhaps cannot, happen and the advocacy is left to those who are inevitably themselves part of the power structures against which they protest – even though they may have genuinely made their 'option for the poor'. There is thus quite a different dynamic at work: it is a difference that goes beyond the conventional contrast between bottom-up development and top-down development. In the process of conscientisation, people discover their own powerlessness and find the resources within themselves and within their group to translate that powerlessness into a readiness to confront abuses of power. In the advocacy model, one group of powerful people confronts another group of even more powerful people and seeks to persuade them to use their power less tyrannically.

Both approaches, however, assume that there is a particular instance or institution that can be confronted. The conscientised poor confront their oppressors. The advocate confronts those who use their superior power oppressively. Suppose, however, that the processes that impoverish the poor are more subterranean, less visible, less palpable than that. Suppose they are even more abstract, more disembodied than the mechanisms identified by the structuralists, like the terms of trade or the transfer of technology. Then it becomes more difficult to think of either advocacy or conscientisation as a correct response.

This is the nature of the challenge posed by a large group of writers on development called the dependency school or, to honour their Latin American origins, the *dependistas*. Rather like the structuralists, the *dependistas* are so diverse in their approach that it is hard to summarise the leading tenets of the school without offending one group or another. I shall make only one crucial distinction, that between Marxist and non-Marxist writers.

The latter, led by André Gunder Frank, argue that the developing world is so dependent upon the metropolitan countries for capital, technology, markets and even for consumer tastes, that the possibilities of authentic development do not exist. Thus in one of his earlier but very important works, Frank rejected modernisation and all its works thus:

> ... underdevelopment is not due to the survival of archaic institutions and the existence of capital shortage in regions that have remained isolated from the stream of world history. On the contrary, underdevelopment was and still is generated by the very same historical process which also generated economic development: the development of capitalism itself...[1]

One of Frank's early followers was, for a time, Colin Leys. In his formative book *Underdevelopment in Kenya,* revealingly sub-titled *The Political Economy of Neo-Colonialism,* he argued that the role of international capital in Kenya would both make a 'genuine' development impossible and lead to increased tension between town and country, and between capital-owners and wage-workers.[2] He therefore had some trenchant things to say about the supposed 'stability' of Kenya – a feature that made that country one of the largest recipients of aid from the Church development agencies throughout the 1960s and 1970s.

Not only is authentic development rendered impossible: un-development or de-development is an inevitable result of relationships that ensure that capital is transferred from the poor countries to the rich. Frank and his disciples showed a number of ways by which this might occur – monopoly profits of transnational corporations, inflated selling prices for capital goods from the rich countries, cheap land grants to foreign investors, agreement between foreign agricultural concerns and local labour élites to keep wages low.

For Frank, the only way forward for the developing, or as he would say, undeveloping, countries is to opt out of the international economic system altogether, as China did after the break with Russia, as Japan did before Captain Perry's intervention, and as Cuba talked about doing after the Bay of Pigs.

In reaching that conclusion, Frank differs from the Marxist *dependistas* who argue that capitalism will expand through the international economy until its own inner contradictions lead it to collapse and be superseded by socialism. For such writers, there is a dimension of historical inevitability about this process.[3] It may be unpleasant and unjust, but it has to be borne until capitalism destroys itself. They argue then that it is pointless for countries to try to escape an unstoppable, unreformable global system: indeed, they express surprise that the progress of capitalism has seemingly been checked in the rural areas of India and Africa, where pre-capitalist systems of economic organisation continue, unexpectedly, to survive.[4]

For both Marxist and non-Marxist *dependistas,* however, the key issue is that international capitalism requires *and therefore creates* a hinterland or periphery which by definition is poorer than the capitalist core, is dependent upon it, and is exploited (in one sense or another) by it. That is to say, *dependistas* see the whole capitalist economic system as one which creates and maintains people on the periphery in poverty.

According to this view, then, the problem to be confronted is not the net that impedes the flow of resources to the poor: it is a huge siphon that extracts 'surplus' from the periphery. The more surplus that is created on the periphery, the more there will be to be extracted. Whether or not it is so extracted will depend on a large number of factors, most notably the degree of penetration of capitalism into the periphery and the manner in which it relates to pre-capitalist institutions and forms of economic organisation. Nonetheless, it follows from this style of analysis that for well-meaning development agencies to create new wealth on the periphery is merely to risk subsidising capitalism at one remove. For the new wealth may be sucked out of the periphery and finally – perhaps after many intermediate transactions – come to rest at the centre of economic power, the great institutions of international financial capital: the multinational banks, the transnational corporations, the international trading houses and the financial professionals that feed upon them.

I hope this short summary of an extremely important corpus of ideas that dominated thinking – or at least non-modernisation thinking – about development from the mid-1960s to the early-1980s reveals its incompatibility with both advocacy models and, less fundamentally perhaps, conscientisation models. If you believe that *capitalism* is the problem, there is not too much point in asking capitalists to be more humane capitalists. There may be some point in encouraging peasants to organise against capitalism, but only if they will create the social and political space to organise a non-capitalist economy of their own.

We need to ask two questions. What truth is there in the *dependista* argument? How did the Churches respond to it? I want to answer those questions with three case studies. I have chosen them because they put these questions – and the whole *dependista* challenge – in a wider context and in a properly rooted experience.

The cases I shall describe are all actual, but they have been fictionalised in order to protect the identity of some of the key participants for reasons that will become obvious.

The first example comes from the Philippines under the Marcos régime. On one of the outlying islands of the Philippines, there has long been a history of conflict between a small number of local oligarchs, who own the sugar and coconut plantations, and the struggling trade union that seeks to represent the workers both on the estates and in the associated mills. The landowners are nominally Roman Catholic, most of the workers are Catholic but there is a significant minority of Moslems. These Moslems tend to be less educated, employed usually on a part-time or seasonal basis, forming to all intents and purposes an underclass.

The Catholic Church can be found on both sides of the sociological divide. The bishop of the area is distantly related to one of the landowners, attended a smart Catholic college and then university in Manila. Although in many ways a good and compassionate man, he has not found developments in Catholic theology and policy since Vatican II easy to swallow. He tended to see the political opposition to the Marcos régime as essentially communist, and therefore inimical to the Church. Perhaps oddly then, his relationship with two of his priests who are working with the trade union movement is nevertheless cordial, pastoral and tolerant. Perhaps he doesn't fully understand their position, either theologically or politically. Essentially paternalistic in his attitude to the poor and the exploited, a little bit of him admires what these two priests are doing, while the ecclesiastical statesman in him pleads for – and practises – caution, gradualism and the avoidance of an open breach with his natural peer group, the landowning classes.

The two priests who work with the trade unions likewise have a soft spot for their bishop. 'We must be thankful that he doesn't actually prohibit us or move us to another part of the diocese,' said one. 'He doesn't support us and he doesn't like to be kept too closely informed about what we are doing, but it is already something that he hasn't moved overtly against us.' For these priests have been deeply affected by liberation theology, which they see as directly applicable to the groups among whom they work. One of them is almost bitter.

'What is the Good News the Church has brought these people over the years?' he asks rhetorically. 'That Christ redeems them from their sins? What does that mean to them? What can redemption mean when they owe a year's wages to the cantina which charges prices twenty per cent above those in the town; when they live in huge communal dormitories that heat up like an oven in the hot weather, with one tap for twenty families, inadequate cooking facilities and filthy lavatories? What is the Good News we bring them when they are paid by the amount of cane that they cut and they know the scales that weigh the cane are rigged against them?'

Starting from a conventional parish ministry, these two priests decided that part of the Good News that they had to bring to these people was the news that the conditions under which they lived and worked were as repugnant to Christ as they are to the workers themselves. They decided that a Gospel that turned a blind and therefore conniving eye at the oppression of the people was a blasphemy. They therefore set about teaching the people to read and write, encouraging them to ask questions about their social conditions. Why do so many young children die? Why can so few parents afford to send their children to school? Why are the prices so much higher in the estate's cantina than they are in the stores in town? Why do five families own all but a tiny proportion of the land in the whole neighbourhood? How would Jesus conduct his ministry in this parish in the light of the answers to these questions?

There were, however, more difficult questions, ones that many faithful Catholics found hard to face. How would Christ react to the Moslems in the area? Would he despise them? Would he be content to see that they got even worse living conditions, even less work, even less access to education and health care? Would Christ's concern be limited to Church-going, faithful Catholics?

Slowly, painfully, out of these questions and the discussions that they began to generate within the community, local leaders began to emerge. It was not long before they began to organise the community, initially round the issue of prices in the cantina and the rate of interest charged on debts by the management of the cantina. This produced a vigorous response from the manager of the estate. He shut the cantina, demanded immediate repayment of all debts and dismissed workers who couldn't pay those debts. The priests tried to raise money from the local community to repay the debts, while the workers themselves tried to prevent other workers accepting employment on the estate. Neither group was successful and many workers lost their jobs, their homes and any chance of permanent employment in the region.

Into this situation came two overseas agencies. They had heard of the wretched conditions of the estate workers and the even more wretched conditions of the fired workers. And they had heard of the pressure that the two priests were under from the local government authorities, the police and directly from the landowners. What could they do?

One of them, a German agency, proposed building a school. That way, they argued, the younger people would acquire an education and would be able to compete for better jobs than working on the estate. The school could be used in the evening for adult education classes or home economics and even some vocational training, to raise the level of skills in the community as a whole. With great enthusiasm, the two young Germans from the agency started sketching out plans and even started negotiating for a site.

It was at that point that some of the workers' leaders started asking hard questions. What 'better jobs' would there be for the children who graduated from the school? They would have to leave the island, perhaps even go to Manila to find such jobs, and was it not common knowledge that unemployment in towns, supremely in Manila, was extremely high? And how would this project benefit the local population in the short-term? All it would do would be to weaken the local community by providing an escape hatch for a limited number of the more talented children.

The Germans reasoned with the recalcitrant villagers, explaining that without education the community was doomed. Certainly the benefits would be some time coming through and probably some children would have to leave in search of better jobs. But that's the process of development at work, they argued. You can't expect every community to develop in isolation from the rest of society. And who knows: the government might build a factory, or the landowner might diversify his crops and put up more processing plants. The Germans continued drawing up their plans...

The other agency, from a small European country, was more sensitive but equally puzzled. They could see the long run potential of the work the priests were doing and they could see that apart perhaps from a typewriter, some stationery and some elementary visual aids, there was little that an external agency could do to help. They told the priests that their agency would almost certainly be prepared to supply the necessary stores, providing an application form could be filled in in triplicate and the duration and results of the programme precisely described.

The night before they left the village, the community gave a party for them. Two families contributed small pigs; other families brewed some coconut wine; even the poorest families contributed rice or tomatoes or oil. The couple from the agency felt ashamed that they could contribute nothing and be recipients only of the generosity of the community.

They decided the only thing they could do was to make one more attempt to find a way of helping the village as generously as the village was treating them. After the feast had been in progress some considerable time, therefore, they spoke to all the villagers again.

'We see how unfairly you are treated', they said, 'and how great are the inequalities in this community. We see that you are almost the slaves of this system, since if you try to leave the work, the landowners will sue you for the debts that you owe at the cantina. You will be imprisoned and worse off than ever. We see that the struggle to organise, so that together you can resist the wealth and the power of the landowners, is going to be long and hard. We want to support you in that struggle. We feel inadequate and guilty that we can think of nothing more to do to help you.'

The villagers were silent for a long time and then a conversation in Tagalog took place which the visitors were not able to understand. The priests were silent throughout this conversation though following it intently.

Eventually one of the leaders stood up and said to the visitors: 'We know that you mean well and that you sincerely want to help us. We value your being here and we value your understanding of our position. But if you really want to help us in the struggle that lies ahead, there is one thing you can do. We know your country is the headquarters of a large and important company that buys sugar and coconut oil on this island. We want you to go to that company and say to it: "We will ask our people not to buy your products unless you, as a company, tell the landowners on this island to treat their workers better".'

Spontaneous applause broke out from the villagers. It was clear that the spokesman had universal support. A number of subsequent speakers reinforced that impression. Eventually an old man, toothless, scrawny and bent, got with difficulty to his feet. 'I say this: you do not break a coconut with a single stick. We are only a small stick. You are a big machete. Between us we can break the coconut. Alone we can never do it. Perhaps the coconut rather will break us.'

The visitors were nonplussed. Were they to tell the truth – that their Council would never agree to such a dialogue, with its implied threat, with one of the biggest companies in the land? Or should they agree to do what they could, knowing that it would be next to nothing, but leave the villagers at least thinking that something would be done? They talked quietly among themselves and finally decided that, whatever else, they had to be truthful.

'We thank you for what you have said and for sharing with us so openly and honestly. As you have been truthful with us, we feel we have to be truthful with you. You say that we are a machete, that we can slice open the coconut if the coconut is held by another stick. You flatter us. We are a small penknife that will be blunted and broken by the husk of the coconut. Indeed, there are many among us who would not want to pick up the penknife to attack the coconut. They prefer to keep the penknife intact and functioning, rather than risk having it made useless.'

The speaker, already taxed to the limit of his facility for analogical conversation, paused to draw breath. In the pause, the old man's voice rang out, shaking with anger.

'What's the use of a penknife, however sharp and well-oiled, if it stays on the shelf? Tell them to go home and not bother us again.'

My second story is from Sri Lanka. It concerns a co-operative producing tea. It was set up after serious disturbances in 1970, primarily for young unemployed school leavers whom the government saw as a potential political threat. The co-operative prospered, not least because it diversified out of tea on some of its land, and replanted most of the original tea estate with new high-yielding hybrid varieties.

By the end of the decade most of the young men who had been settled on the co-operative had married and started families. Some had three or four children. They had organised a primary school with help from the government. Most promising of all, they were beginning to build their own tea factory. They had a contract with a European alternative marketing organisation to supply packeted tea, thus raising the value of their crop. They hoped thereby to create livelihoods for more people in the co-operative. That contract could only become effective, however, when the new factory was built. Getting it built was therefore a high priority for the whole co-operative.

At a critical stage, the international tea market collapsed. The price received by the co-operative for tea auctioned in Colombo fell thirty per cent in ten months. The income it was now receiving barely paid the fixed costs of the co-operative. Members took swingeing cuts in the wages they paid themselves and work on the new factory was stopped. Worse, some of the materials that had been bought had to be sold in order to prevent the co-operative going into debt.

The alternative marketing organisation that had been

planning to buy packeted tea from the co-operative received this letter.

Dear Friends,
We are sorry to say that this letter brings bad news. The Colombo tea auctions show no sign of improving. If anything, we are told to expect prices to go even lower. We still have some of last season's tea to sell and we are beginning to wonder whether it is even worth taking it down to the floor. (i.e. the auction floor.)

When you came to talk to us about your organisation and the way in which you hoped to be able to pay a fair price for our tea, we were filled with hope. But now it is as though the train has pulled out of the station just as we were running on to the platform. We have had to suspend work on the factory and it doesn't look as if we shall be able to start for a year or two at least.

This makes us ask deeper questions. You were kind enough to offer us a contract and deliver us from the madness of prices that swing about all over the place and which even at their best barely afford us a reasonable living. We would like to accept that offer. It offered us a way out.

But now we ask ourselves whether we are justified in taking that way out. What about every other co-operative on the island, or even worse, the workers on the estates? All of us involved in growing tea are caught in a system that is as unstable as it is unjust.

We know that you, by offering an alternative marketing channel, are pointing out some of the absurdities and the inequities of the existing system. That is why we went along with you, quite apart from our own self-interest. But is that enough? Is it enough if it only reaches one per cent or even five per cent of the growers? Surely what you ought to be doing is working to transform the whole of the tea trade. For ourselves, we find that we cannot, in good conscience, take advantage of a more favourable deal that is restricted to us while others are caught in the existing market system.

We hope you understand our position and do not think too ill of us. Perhaps one day you will see that it would be quite wrong of us to offer you an easy salve to your conscience while the majority of our fellow countrymen employed in this industry suffer the near catastrophe of the last fifteen months – a catastrophe which will be repeated, as it has been in the past, again and again in the future.

The recipients of this letter were deeply disturbed. They felt their Sri Lankan partners were letting them down and were judging them harshly. Was it not the case, they asked, that by providing an alternative marketing outlet, they were revealing the inadequacies and inequities of the conventional market? It was naive of the Sri Lankan co-operative to expect them to be able to change the whole face of tea marketing in Europe when their total turnover was less than a million pounds a year. They were doing their very best and in time, no doubt, they would be able to persuade more people to pay a premium price for the satisfaction of knowing that they were not part of an exploitative international system.

Surely, they argued, the Sri Lankans could see that the changing consciousness of European consumers could only be brought about gradually and through education, through example, through building up a genuine alternative to the big international combines that dominate the tea trade. It was unrealistic for the Sri Lankans to expect them to take on those combines, not least because as one of the senior staff members put it, 'the market is the market'. The price slump had been brought about by record crops in India, Kenya and Sri Lanka itself, reduced purchases in the Middle East and Russia, and a stagnant market in Europe and the United States. 'What more, for Pete's sake,' said the same staff member, 'do they expect us to do?'

These two stories have a common theme, namely that local communities of poor people are not divorced or insulated from the abuse of power within the international economy. The wider international context may be mediated in quite different ways but the message is clear: what these particular people were looking for was less project assistance or funding than deliverance from an international economy which they experience as harmful or destructive. The final story – no less true and no less fictionalised than the others – takes that a step further.

As is well known and much appreciated, the voluntary agencies played a significant role in the introduction of new high-yielding varieties of rice and wheat in the Ganges Plain in North India. Substantial sums of money from the voluntary sector, particularly but by no means exclusively from the United States, were invested in tubewells, generators, draught oxen, storage and marketing facilities. Although much conventional wisdom suggested that the agricultural progress associated with these improvements would be confined to middle and larger scale farmers, experience showed that even very small scale farmers were able to benefit from the new technology, not least because the development agencies, acting in association with Indian voluntary organisations, were able to help the poorest to acquire the necessary inputs.

Near the town of Kanpur in Uttar Pradesh, a group of donors, in association with an Indian Church development agency, was involved in financing a rural development project which included not only the adoption of the new varieties of rice, but also health care, education, access to drinking water, house building and what in India is known as village improvement. In the mid 1970s, the project seemed to be going well. Output was up. Living standards, particularly of some of the smaller farmers, were improving. Slowly and sometimes with setbacks, the infrastructure associated with the project was put in place.

Some of the smaller farmers were now getting two or even two and a half crops a year and their income was rising sharply. Some of them were able to rent-in new land and the size of their holdings increased. As that happened, so they found they were short of labour. Whereas the family had sufficed to cultivate three hectares, additional labour was required when the farm expanded to six or eight hectares. Labour began to be in short supply and therefore in peak periods – during transplanting and harvesting in particular – wages rose to hitherto undreamt of levels. Seasonal workers began to migrate into the area from Rajasthan to the west and from Madya Pradesh in the south.

It was at this point that a number of farmers, led by some of the larger scale farmers but also including some of the smaller farmers who had been part of the original development project, began to take an interest in modern agricultural equipment.

The biggest farmers started to talk of combine harvesters: even the smaller farmers of mechanical threshers and hand-held tractors. That way, they argued, they could save on wages and be spared reliance on uncertain and generally disliked migrant labour.

By some strange process of telepathy or osmosis, a Belgian agricultural equipment salesman appeared in the area. He assured the farmers they would have no trouble getting foreign exchange to import his machinery, since the Belgian government would finance it through a variety of export subsidies and aid.

Worried about their capacity to withstand further indebtedness at the high rates of interest they would have to pay in the village, a number of the smaller farmers came to the project manager asking for loans with which to buy the imported machinery. The project had, after all, given them loans for pumps, for generators, even for trucks. Why should they be difficult about loans for other forms of equipment which would make the farms even more profitable?

Needless to say, the project manager didn't see matters in quite that light. Much of the new equipment was designed to save labour, that is to deprive poor people – migrants or local – of livelihoods and force down the general level of wages. How could that possibly be consistent with a project that was designed to raise the standards of living of poor people?

Others in the project team argued differently. They pointed out that Indian agriculture could only prosper if output per acre and output per head were to rise. Deliberately to hold back the economic progress of some of the most successful farms on the project would be to risk losing all credibility.

It was at this point that the local community became involved. The small farmers were outraged that the project should demur. The landless workers, including the seasonal migrants, were predictably quick to see the implications of what was afoot and were consequently no less outraged that the project should even consider undercutting their livelihood. Indeed, they demanded that the project personnel join them in violent demonstrations against some of the larger landowners whose capacity for labour saving was most marked.

In the end, the pressures blew the project to bits. Some of the major landowners feared that the project staff would try to prevent the importation of the machinery and they therefore used their influence with the state government to have all expatriate staff banned from the project. One direct consequence was that the transfer of funds became so entwined with bureaucratic red tape that the project's survival became problematic. At the same time, the landless and seasonal workers became increasingly suspicious of the project, claiming that it was in league with the more successful farmers. Whatever its stance on this particular issue, they argued, it would always favour the more successful farmers – i.e. those who could profitably adopt the new technology – against the really poor. In the end the project collapsed – unloved, universally reviled, and wholly unlamented.

These three case studies – true, it is worth emphasising, in their main features – point out not only the limits of the project system, but also the inescapable impact of metropolitan conditions on villages, even remote villages, in the developing world. That impact is mediated in a number of ways, most of them associated in one way or another with the mechanisms of international trade. In so far as dependency theory points out that those mechanisms can and often do reduce levels of living in the poor countries, it is hard to gainsay it. The locus of that effect, however, lies less in the *dependent* nature of the poor countries than in the unequal power relationships upon which international trade is built, and which it maintains in the poor countries themselves. In the Philippines the international sugar industry creates and maintains the system against which the people were rebelling, and it plays its part in maintaining a government and political culture which secures its own perpetuation. In Sri Lanka the co-operative is caught by an inherently unstable market which producer and consumer countries have failed to reform (and which Britain, as a leading consumer, has consistently denied needs reforming). In India, class differences within rural society are aggravated by the aggressive promotion of a technology that brings great individual benefits – but even greater social costs.

In each case the victims of the system are not in a position to resist or much affect the pressures which increase their poverty. The Filipinos cannot alter the structure of the sugar industry –

nor, in this case, can the donor agency. The Sri Lankans cannot change the way the tea-market operates – their European friends can insulate them from its effects, but only them. The landless labourers in India cannot change the self-interest of the larger farmers, nor resist the sales force of the Belgian exporter.

The victims are powerless. So too are the project agencies to which they relate. The agencies may come from the same country, the same political culture as the 'oppressor', but they can do nothing to bring to an end their oppression. *Dependistas* would not be surprised by this fact. Locating 'the problem' in the nature and process of international capital accumulation, they would point out that the agencies are so on the fringes of that process that *by their very nature* they are incapable of tackling the roots of poverty, or rather of impoverishment. Some *dependistas* would indeed argue that the agencies make things worse in two ways. They obscure the real processes at work and thus make it harder for progressive forces to mobilise. And by increasing to however small a degree the surplus available, they actually subsidise the capital accumulation of international financial institutions.

My argument is different. I acknowledge the very far-reaching impact of our culture on the life chances and political processes of vast areas of the developing world. That impact contains both good and ill, though often the latter is less immediately obvious than the former. Indeed, in much of its work in development, the Church has sought to maximise that good on the more visible level while leaving unchallenged the ill at the deeper level. The Germans building the school in the Philippines is almost a classic example of this phenomenon. When the Church has tried to tackle some of the deeper underlying problems, as in the case of the alternative marketing organisation selling the co-operative's tea in Sri Lanka, what it has been able to do has been so small, so tangential to the fundamental issues that it has sometimes spread despair rather than hope in the developing countries concerned.

It is important that the argument not be misunderstood at this point. For we are now at the core of the book. What I have tried to show, both in analysis and in anecdote, is that the

Churches have over-invested in approaches to development that are not necessarily destructive or unnecessary, but which are inadequate by themselves and which are very easily subverted into countersigns. The school becomes a school for the élite. The agricultural project becomes an agricultural project for the successful, progressive farmer. The hospital becomes a disease palace. The Church development office becomes another middle-class, top-down bureaucracy. That is not to deny that they do a perfectly respectable job and a job that perhaps has to be done. It is, however, to call in question whether that is the real vocation of the Church, and whether it is likely to produce an authentic pattern of development which fully reflects biblical understandings of the nature of man and of society.

The great popularity accorded to conscientisation/liberation theology has had the effect of reinforcing the assumption – which metropolitan Churches find convenient to leave in place – that development is a matter for the developing countries. According to this view, it is the role of the Churches in the metropolitan countries to support the efforts of the Church development agencies in the developing countries with money, training and manpower. In other words, both the modern-isation paradigm and the conscientisation/liberation para-digm have this in common: they situate the most effective point of engagement for the metropolitan Churches in the develop-ing countries themselves.

Like the *dependistas*, I believe that to be a fundamental error. Unlike them, however, I would argue that the rich and poor worlds will always be inter-dependent and that that relationship of inter-dependence will always be unequal. Because it *is* unequal, the rich and the powerful will always seek to exploit it to their own advantage. The ontological basis of that is not, *pace* the *dependistas*, in capitalism: it is in human nature. It will be true, therefore, irrespective of the nature of economic organisation in the rich countries. (It *may* be true that in a socialist north there would be more natural sympathy for the victims of the process, though the record of the USSR does not inspire much confidence.) I do not regard forms of economic organisation as definitive. What is definitive is the *level and nature of the consciousness that informs the actions of the rich and powerful in their dealings with the relatively poor and relatively powerless.*

It is the creation of an *alternative* consciousness, which in the spirit of magnificat and beatitude puts the poor and the powerless at its centre, that is the true task of the Church in development. This alternative consciousness is not paternalistic or condescending: it is a consciousness that turns upside down the priorities and assumptions of twentieth century industrialised, secularised acquisitiveness (whether capitalist or socialist) and judges relationships, structures, and economic ties not by what profit it brings to the dominant partner but by how much it enlarges the life chances of the subordinate partner. That means the judgments have to be made by the subordinate partner – which in turn means that the subordination is ended. The interests of the poor and powerless, as formulated and expressed by them themselves, thus become definitive of the alternative consciousness. The rich and powerful, in other words, have to learn to use their wealth and power not for their own aggrandisement, but for the goals set by the poor and powerless.

And that is metanoia. Conversion. Revolution. Gospel. We need to explore it further in the remainder of this book.

Chapter 9

1 Power and Powers in the Bible

At each stage in the argument of this book we have seen how asymmetrical power is a fundamental, perhaps *the* fundamental, principle that maintains processes of impoverishment. I have argued that asymmetrical power operates at many levels – from the international to the village – and that it also permeates the life of the Church, in racism and sexism, as well as the relationships between the donor agencies of the North and their clients (however structured) in the South. It is that asymmetrical power that has to be transformed by what I have called alternative consciousness. As I have already hinted, the acquisition and sharing of that consciousness ('conversion' and 'evangelism') are deeply religious experiences. For the Christian they are Christ-centred, the subjection of the ego, whether individual or corporate, to the liberating discipline of the dying and rising Christ who makes all things new.

I shall start by giving a few signposts to biblical understandings of power and I shall then try to apply that to the subject matter of the preceding chapters. We shall find, however, that we are caught in a two-way process, a dialectical relationship between the outward, material world and the inner, spiritual world. I shall repeatedly emphasise, therefore – as I do now – that we are dealing with *one* reality: the outward does not exist apart from the inward; and the inward is always incorporated, enfleshed, made meat in the outward.

Given the wealth of power-language in the New Testament it is odd indeed that Christians have been so loath to come to terms with the significance of power for understandings of the life, death and resurrection of Jesus Christ. Walter Wink, for example, points to thirteen *pairs* of words for power (and its cognates such as authority, ruler) – and emphasises that most of them appear, not as one might expect in the Pauline epistles, but in the Gospels and Acts.[1] Power then is not a concept the Bible is frightened of confronting. Indeed, Wink shows that the New Testament has a coherent and very 'modern' appreciation of the pervasiveness, moral ambiguity and concreteness of power.

We need, first, to sketch in, albeit in the most tentative outline, some of the Old Testament background. The central fact about the way the Old Testament sees power, authority, dominion is that they belong ultimately to Yahweh (Ps. 62:11). Six of the seven references to power in the Psalms repeat the same point: it is God's and his alone. He demonstrates it in love towards his people, in creation and in freeing them from bondage in Egypt (Exod. 15:6).

It is this fact, that Yahweh uses his power for the greater good of his people, that becomes determinative of the nature of the Covenant, and therefore of the nature of Old Testament religion. In the Covenant Yahweh, as it were, pledges his power to that end: that is his side of the bargain. If the people break the Covenant, then Yahweh is free to use his power against them, to bring them to repentance and a reconstitution of the morality of the Covenant. Ideally, then, power is used to assure fruitfulness, peace, harmony, stability – all that the Old Testament understands by wholeness and holiness. Rewards of the just keeping of the Covenant will be guaranteed by Yahweh's power, as surely as punishment will be meted out by that same power when the Covenant is broken.

It is no surprise, for example, to find that spelled out at the end of the Law of Holiness:

If you conform to my statutes, if you observe my commandments and carry them out, I will give you rain at the proper times: the land shall yield its produce, and the trees of the countryside bear fruit. Threshing shall last till vintage and vintage till sowing: you shall eat your fill and live secure in your land. I will give peace in the land and you shall lie down to sleep with no one to terrify you ... If after all this you do not listen to me, I will go on to punish you seven times over for your sins. I will break down your stubborn pride (or, in the AV, I will break down your power). I will make the sky above you like iron and the earth beneath you like bronze. Your strength shall be spent in vain: your land shall not yield its produce nor the trees of the land bear fruit (Lev. 26:3–20).

Here we get a glimpse of the possibilities of humanity's counter-vailing power. It is hinted that humanity can use its power to vaunt its independence, to go its own way in defiance of the Covenant; or it can choose to use it in a way that enables the Covenant to be lived out, to become a reality in the whole of the life of the people of God. I put it in that rather clumsy language to underline the fact that to the writers of the Moses tradition our separation of secular and sacred would have been either meaningless or blasphemous. Power was a category that applied to both secular and sacred (in our terminology), to every aspect of every relationship. Abuse of power was thus an abuse of Yahweh's righteousness, whether the immediate victim was widow, stranger, orphan or working mule. The idea that power could be used in one 'kingdom' without having immediate implications for the quality of relationship in the other – an idea that was to wreak such havoc in post-Reformation times – is an idea so alien to the Old Testament that it is no surprise that it depends exclusively on New Testament (and above all on Pauline) passages and their Greek notions of philosophy and ethics.

As Yahweh uses his power to guarantee the Covenant, then, so humankind is to use its power to actualise the quality of life promised by the Covenant. That parallel is crucial. What gives Yahweh's power moral status is, first, his role of Creator and second (derived from the nature of that creative act) the fact that Yahweh's power is used to bring about his people's deepest *corporate* self-fulfilment. It is the guarantee of community wholeness. It is the guarantee of justice between weak and strong. It undergirds right-dealing and peace (Ps. 94: Job 37:23–4). In exactly the same way, those who exercise earthly power, authority, have moral status only in so far as they use that power to those ends.

'Yahweh repays me as I act justly, as my purity is in his sight. Faithful you are with the faithful, blameless with the blameless', sings David in 2 Samuel 22:25–26, and he goes on to ascribe the military and political success of his reign to the fact that he has used his power in conformity with Yahweh's covenant-love. That may seem an arrogant or even farcical claim in the light of the historical record: but it reveals an acknowledgement in the community out of which this 'Davidic' psalm came that the moral basis of power is faithfulness to the Covenant.[2]

The Old Testament presents the history of Israel as the history of its rulers' loyalty to the Covenant and to the monotheism defined therein. For it is when they encourage idolatry that the rulers are denying the source of their own power – and the moral quest that lies behind that power. Jehovah is a jealous God precisely because the idols cannot create the social, economic and religious conditions under which Israel can prosper and find peace in the deepest and richest senses of *Shalom*. Idolatry is therefore always damnable: it is particularly damnable when it stems from the abuse of a power bestowed in order to make possible what idolatry denies.

It is in this sense that power and salvation are linked. The power of Yahweh guarantees and undergirds the Covenant. The power of Yahweh enables the kings and rulers to protect and give existential embodiment to the Covenant, and it is in that embodiment that salvation consists. For salvation is the wholeness of human activity, the wholeness of human relationship and the wholeness of human community. And it is precisely the function of political power, derived directly in the Old Testament tradition from Yahweh, to make that wholeness possible. The full wrath of the eighth-century prophets is thus directed against rulers who use their power for lesser purposes or for a distortion of those purposes. Cultic ritual has to be brought under judgment because it no longer gives existential expression to the nature and quality of the Covenant relationship. Abuses of kingly power have to be brought under judgment precisely because they deny the quality of the relationship guaranteed in the Covenant by Yahweh. Idolatry is condemned because it makes impossible the fullness into which Yahweh is calling his people, and ascribes saving power to phenomena that have no saving power.

With that theme, however, goes another – more elusive, more subtle, more challenging. It is in counterpoint to the theology of kingly power, for it sees power from the standpoint of the victim of the abuse of power. The Suffering Servant of Second Isaiah, however, not only bears the pains of power misused; he does so in a way that liberates others, possibly including those who abuse him. 'Through his wounds, we are healed' (Isa. 53:5). The Servant judges kingly power not by punishing it or resisting it with physical force, but by allowing it to do its worst (Isa. 53:8).

> ... So disfigured did he look
> that he seemed no longer human...
> ... kings stand speechless before him...
> 'Who could believe what we have heard
> and to whom has the power of Yahweh been revealed?'
> (Isa. 52:14–53:1)

Paradoxically the power of Yahweh is revealed in the suffering of this innocent servant, suffering to the point of death, to bring peace and healing for all those who had gone astray from the Covenant relationship. Yahweh's power thus has a double reference: it is demonstrated in nature and politics as a power to make the Covenant live. But it is demonstrated too as redemptive suffering, to heal the breaches inflicted on the Covenant relationship by the sinfulness of the Covenant people.

In the Gospels, Jesus maintains both these traditions. The 'authority' with which he teaches about the Kingdom (Mark 1:22) is the announcement of God's salvation, God's wholeness, for those who have been denied it by the worldly powers of State and Sanhedrin. 'Therefore this power of Jesus stands in irreconcilable opposition to every metaphysical glorification of human, political powers, and in the same way to the claim of a theocracy that by appeal to God's lordship wants only to press its own demand for power'.[3] In this sense, Jesus is a powerful figure of authority, daring, in Ernst Fuchs' revealing phrase, 'to act in God's stead'.[4] He acts, of course, in conformity with the Covenant, bringing loving generosity to those excluded or persecuted by the existing power structures. He turns upside down much contemporary dogma and ethics (Matt. 5:21–33); surrounds himself with the off-scourings of his own society, thereby repudiating actions of purity and cleanliness that were divorced from loving care, and fulfills the prophetic promise of the inbreaking of the Kingdom of God by healing the blind, deaf and sick.

It is in this context of great authority – the authority of the Old Testament expectations brought to a startling reality – that Jesus's powerlessness has to be set. Jenkins and Moltmann are right, no doubt, to put great emphasis on the determination with which Jesus resists earthly power – for example in the account of the Temptations or, more overtly, in the attempt to persuade him to lead a rebellion against Rome.[5] He not only resists such power; he stands it on its head. Placed significantly by Luke at the end of his account of the Last Supper, Jesus tells his power-grabbing disciples that his way, their way, is quite different: 'Let the greatest among you become... as one who serves' (Luke 22:25–7). The Servant theme is restated and Jesus lives out its judgment on kingly power by refusing to save himself from the Cross. Most revealingly, in the Markan account (which contains a wealth of material on this theme) it is an unnamed woman who sees Jesus's real identity, and anoints him 'as both king in his death... and as the needy corpse... It is in his powerlessness that he is king...'[6] The powers of the world, it seems, finally assert their superiority over the authority of God.

That we need to honour Jesus's powerlessness and learn deeply from it, I do not deny. There is, however, a danger in so emphasising that deliberate putting-off of power, his *kenosis*, that we ignore the setting in which it is placed – the real exercise of prophetic authority 'in God's stead'. An exclusive concern with powerlessness can reinforce a tendency that we modern Christians already have – to exaggerate our own powerlessness *vis-à-vis* the powers of the world and justify that exaggeration by a false self-identification with the powerlessness of Christ. At its least harmful, this is merely a cop-out; at its most harmful it is a more or less conscious process of collusion with the powers that Jesus came to judge. Nothing could be further removed from the realities of his ministry. How, then, to hold in proper tension his prophetic authority with his acceptance of the tradition of the Suffering Servant in the use of earthly power against himself? That is a question to which we shall have to turn in the next chapter: for the moment, we need to take the New Testament evidence two steps further.

First, it is important surely to put the crucifixion, the apotheosis of powerlessness, into its total revelatory context – as, incidentally, St Paul usually does when writing about the Cross. The Cross is followed by the Resurrection, from our point of view a devastating act of the power of God. However much mythological load one accords our 'historical' accounts of the resurrection, the biblical record is clear: he who had been declared accursed and killed by the powers of the world is proved alive and life-giving in the experience of those who declare their allegiance to his ultimate authority, his Lordship. The power of God to judge the judges, to reverse the verdict of those who abuse their own (derivative) power by obstructing the creation of Covenant relationships – that power is mightily asserted, in both resurrection and pentecost. (The relationship between those 'events' is, of course, much debated by theologians; whatever the historical relationship, the core of my argument here is unaffected.)

It is thus no surprise to find that the power of the Spirit brings with it a new spring of Covenant-relationship. The sick are cured. Goods are shared. Harmony and serenity are lived out. The poor hear the good news of peace and justice and wholeness.

It looks as though the Kingdom, God's rule, has indeed come among his people (Acts 2:42–3:10). It is, of course, very different from the Kingdom foreshadowed in Jewish apocalyptic, but it is recognisably, at least to the eye of faith of the early Christians viewing it from the inside, coherent with the Kingdom Jesus proclaimed – and which his disciples expected to see him usher in from a position of authority (Luke 22:30). Yet the community of the Kingdom remains pathetically small, even if we believe the probably exaggerated accounts of the rate of growth of the early Church. Not only does it remain numerically small, geographically scattered and soon deeply divided, but it seems to recruit most of its membership from the uneducated and not-too-respectable segments of society. An odd Kingdom, then; a Kingdom in embryo, in chrysalis, waiting to be perfected. The marks of the Kingdom, a share in Christ's death and resurrection through baptism, are however objectively present; and the fruits of the Kingdom, both personal and institutional, are visible to those who have eyes to see (Acts 4:36–5:11).

And yet the powers remain unconverted. The same drab, cruel world refuses to respond with joy and gladness to the news the early Church tries to share. They are in the grip of something demonic that will not allow them to hear the news or respond to it. Caught by forces of evil they cannot counter from their own resources, they remain trapped in their opposition: and they demonstrate that opposition by their continued abuse of their own power against those who would set them free.

In crude outline, such seems to be the position of the Pauline (in the conventional sense) epistles. Walter Wink's important study enables us to go a little further. According to Wink, the 'principalities and powers are the inner spiritual essence or *Gestalt* of an institution or state or system... the "demons" are the psychic or spiritual power emanated by organisations or individuals or subaspects of individuals whose energies are bent on overpowering others – "Satan" is the actual power that congeals around collective idolatry, injustice or inhumanity, a power that increases or decreases according to the degree of collective refusal to choose higher values.'[7]

Power in the sense in which I have used the term so far in this book – the power of the rural élite or of international capital or of the Church – is thus the outward expression, the behaviour pattern towards others, of an 'inner or spiritual essence'. The New Testament therefore reminds us that what is *ultimately* significant is less the power of an institution or system or corporation in an outward sense – what it can do to others; more, its inner wells of motivation and consciousness which make it use its power in a given (egocentric) way. It insists that all created things – individual or collective – have this consciousness or inner essence and that it is *at that level* where liberation and redemption have to be achieved. This comes as both a reminder to our generation of the reductionist fallacy of reducing institutions and systems to the observable realities of the organogram or the political analyst; and a translation into another mode of discourse of Jung's insights into the importance of the collective unconscious.

For the inner essence may not, *pace* the parallel I drew in the last paragraph, be fully conscious. Both individuals and corporations and institutions are subject to a kind of knee-jerk reaction or Pavlovian response that may not be fully conscious. A multinational corporation seeks to buy cheap and sell dear, or to extend its monopoly power not (only) because there are grasping men and women making profit maximising decisions, but because that is the sort of creature it is. That is its essence – and it becomes, perhaps only quarter-consciously, the essence of the people who make it up. In the same way a totalitarian state can hardly *help* being repressive of dissidence or nervous of free artistic expression. It is the spirit of such a régime to use civil power in a certain way. The spirit of the collective moulds the spirit of its officers, as surely as the reverse process operates. No wonder the Christians at Colossae were warned to be on their guard 'against the elemental spirits of the universe'. They were reminded that they had died with Christ and therefore 'passed beyond the reach of the elemental spirits of the universe' (Col. 2:8–20).

It seems to be the Pauline view (accepting conventional notions of authorship of the epistles) that the spirits or powers that control humans and their various orders of collective entities have not been exposed to God's final power, as revealed in the dead and resurrected Son of God. Having written of his gospel – 'Christ nailed to the cross' – Paul goes on to tell the Corinthians: 'I speak God's hidden wisdom, his secret purpose framed from the very beginning to bring us to our full glory. The powers that rule the world have never known it: if they had, they would not have crucified the Lord of glory' (1 Cor. 2:2, 7–9).

Because the powers of the world have never been exposed to the final paradox of power – that it is to be used not for itself but to live out the Covenant for the whole of creation – power is continually misused, abused. It is only when the powers are brought to a knowledge of the paradox of power that they are convicted and our rescue is secured (Col. 1:13). In that sense Christ holds all things together (Col. 1:18) for 'through him God chose to reconcile the whole universe to himself making peace through the shedding of his blood upon the Cross – to reconcile all things whether on earth or in heaven through him alone' (Col. 1:19–20).

Cross and Resurrection thus demonstrate the moral culpability of the powers – and of the way the powers abuse and distort the power of the individuals or collectives in which they are set. In that sense, Christ has been enthroned 'far above all government and authority, all power and dominion...' (Eph. 1:21).

Central to this gospel, then, is the life, death and resurrection of Christ and his victory over the powers of this world and of death itself. For the inner meaning, at the level of the essence of things, of this history is that the powers can be redeemed, can be set free from all that destroys and dehumanises them and others, that power can be used creatively and liberatingly once its controlling Powers are exposed to Christ and his story.

And the central theme of that story, symbolised by the Cross, is that love absorbs abuses of power – and in that process judges them. That love is the love of God in Christ, the powerless love that allows the power of the powerful to do its work, and makes a new beginning possible. Recent history has produced a crop of examples – from Mahatma Gandhi to Martin Luther King to Jawani Luwum to Ed de la Torre. The absorption of the power of the powerful does not lead to the immediate overthrow of the emperor or the dictator; but it reveals the limits of his authority, the unpalatable fact that persecution or violence or imprisonment *can* enforce an outward bending to the will of the powerful, but it cannot break the final allegiance of selfless love. In the end, that final allegiance will conquer the power of the powerful. Thus in the Revelation of St John the Divine, the great drama of Jerusalem and Babylon – a drama in which the powers of life are challenged by the powers of death – ends with a paean of praise for the Lamb. It is the Lamb that is sacrificed who brings Jerusalem to victory. And it is that observation that makes for the whole of the literature of the early Church, and particularly for Revelation, the capacity to endure, the refusal to be overthrown by evil and violence, one of the great Christian virtues.

It is the task, the dangerous, costly, killing task of the Church to ensure that power and its Powers are exposed to this story. Having recalled the seeming futility of the early martyrs challenging the power of the Roman state, Wink continues: 'Then, "Jesus is Lord" shook the foundations of an empire; in the "free" world today, "Jesus is Lord" bumper stickers usually occasion yawns. Cars adorned with them are not stopped at police roadblocks or firebombed by para-military saboteurs. The only people scandalised by the phrase are those who regard its language as sexist. But there are countries where "Jesus, friend of the poor" can get you killed. Fidelity to the gospel lies not in repeating its slogans but in plunging the prevailing idolatries into its corrosive acids. We must learn to address the spirituality of institutions, as well as their visible manifestations, with the ultimate claim of the Ultimate Human.'[8]

For it is with ultimates that we are concerned, and it is that which makes this area of discussion unfamiliar. We largely lack a vocabulary with which to tackle it. At the risk of being crude, I want to try to sketch out where I think the foregoing considerations lead us.

First we need to recognise three levels of analysis – and of activity: the individual; the social and the cosmic. At each level, two seemingly contradictory statements are true: one, demonic forces are at work and can triumph provisionally; two, Christ's death and resurrection objectively determines that those demonic forces will not finally and utterly have their way at any of the three levels. In this sense, the demonic forces are at war with the saving, whole-making, health-inducing, community-upholding energies of Christ, manifested most completely in a death of love on the Cross, and validated by the resurrection life of the first community.

This neat analytical distinction is, however, too neat. For it implies that the three ontological levels – individual, collective and cosmic – are independent. They are, of course, nothing of the sort. They interact with each other constantly and confusingly, so that identifying the Powers that determine their inner essence and on which the demonic forces act is a hard business.

Furthermore, when we put any one level under the microscope we find it disaggregates, in much the same way as a plant tissue or a piece of metal is revealed to be composed of millions of particles when seen under great magnification. Our personalities turn out to be comprised of many 'persons'. Our social structures have their own corporate personality, but are also made up of individuals acting upon each other – and influencing and being influenced by the corporate personality of the institution. Our cosmos is manifestly multiple, comprised of elements that only saints and poets can glimpse as a unity.

Describing the interaction between these three levels in a way that takes seriously the sub-strata of spiritual essence is no easy task. It is indeed one beset by theological, philosophical and existential booby-traps, a reflection which may explain why it is largely uncharted territory. Fools rush in...

Yet the issues are so central not only to our present undertaking but, I believe, to the whole malaise of Western intellectual effort (and supremely theological effort), that, fool or not, I want to try to put the last paragraphs to a simple existential test. Taking a familiar, everyday process – say going to the store to do the family shopping – can I give an account of the Powers at the three levels I have described that sheds any light at all on the main thrust of this book? It is for the reader to judge the next section in that light.

2 Living it Out – Choices

We need to start by recognising that the name of each of us is legion. It is not only that we all have many roles as mother, businessman, member of the Church council, treasurer of the parent teachers association, or whatever it may be. More than that, we are each host to a number of persons. Some of these will seem very negative – the bully, the authority figure, the destroyer – and some will seem either neutral or positively benign – the gardener, the provider, the artist, the carer. Although it takes the deep inward journey, perhaps lasting a lifetime, to recognise and come to terms with these different personas within us, each of them comes with us on our outward journey to confront the Powers of institutions and structures. Our individuality is, as it were, a minibus in which each of our legion of persons rides around with us.

The outward journey then involves the self, but it is a social self set in a variety of social groupings, and it is a self that offers a ride to a variety of persons within its individual minibus. This self has the power of choice. The inner spirit of the self is expressed through the exercise of that choice. That is what gives the self (whether individual or corporate) peculiar value and peculiar status. Certainly some people's power of choice is greater than others – a millionaire can choose what a pauper can't. At a deeper level, however, all individuals and collectives find themselves confronted with the process of discovering who they are as they exercise life's choices. As they make those choices, they both discover who they are and they demonstrate who they are. They reveal the nature of the Powers they incarnate.

Now many of these life's choices are extremely mundane. Very rarely do we have to decide who to marry or whether to change our jobs, whether to develop a new technology or rig a market. The vast majority of our choices are at a much lower level of significance, but taken in aggregate they say a great deal both about the composition of the passengers in the minibus and therefore about this particular self as an individual – and about this firm, or club, or union, or nation, as an aggregation of individuals. Let's look a little closer at some of these choices.

The vast majority of choices, of the exercises of power to choose, impinge on the social domain. Very few choices are purely private. Even what look like private choices often turn out, on closer examination, to have a social dimension. It may seem, for instance, a private choice whether I eat canned tropical fruit produced by a notorious multinational company. Whose business is it but mine? A moment's reflection, however, reveals that that choice is profoundly social. If the multinational concerned is using land that could be growing food for local people, or is using an inappropriate technology that deprives people of jobs, or is investing heavily in countries where repression is used to force down wages, then the power to decide whether or not to buy that company's product, and thereby encourage its activities, clearly has a social dimension.

Sure, a one-person boycott is not going to change the policies of a huge American multinational corporation. That fact alone, however, in no way detracts from the social dimension of the individual decision. We see that perhaps more clearly when we think of a decision by the purchasing manager of a large chain-store. He is not buying a tin of pineapple segments. He is buying tons of pineapple segments, and if a dozen of his opposite numbers in chain-stores take the same decision, the multinational concerned may well begin to re-examine some of its policies. The way British chain-stores began to reassess their sale of South African goods after the picket of Dunn's Stores in Eire is a case in point.

Choices about consumption, however, go much deeper, as the life-style movement, the Greens, and many of the alternative consumption groups constantly remind us. 'We are what we consume' – a challenging exaggeration perhaps, but one that reminds us that, particularly in the rich North, the power represented by the capacity to choose patterns of consumption, life-styles, levels of expectation, constantly need to be subjected to a radical critique from the standpoint of what is just in the light of the absolute poverty of eight hundred million people.

The power to choose consumption patterns, both in terms of level and composition, is not just a private choice designed to titillate the individual palate or maximise the enjoyment of the corporate consumer, but is a way in which both the consumers' Powers are revealed and the producers' Powers are confronted. It is then a point at which inward and outward journeys converge. And they converge not (only) in the huge issues of the Civil Rights movement or the ending of apartheid, but in the stuff of everyday life.

It is there, however, that most of us discover a flaming row going on in the minibus. To stick with the consumption example, some parts of me want radically to simplify my life-style, to express solidarity with the poor by 'letting go' of my high consumption way of life. Part of me clearly hears the classical Christian doctrine on poverty with its emphasis on the creative possibilities of being free of possessions, mortgages, insurance premiums and all the overburden of financial anxiety with which we surround ourselves in an attempt to secure financial security. Some in the minibus are very clear that only when I let go of even the desire for financial security will I discover the fraternity and conviviality which, as Leonardo Boff reminds us, is the essence of Franciscan spirituality.[9] Only then, those voices say, will it really make any existential sense to talk about an alternative consciousness that confronts the Powers of materialism. For unless that alternative consciousness is rooted in such fraternity with the poor, it is no more than a middle class fad, the kind of bourgeois self-indulgence that may go a little way to allay guilt, but goes no way to secure the radical reordering that is the object of alternative consciousness.

Not everyone on the minibus agrees. There are sensible

voices that point out the need for a certain comfort and freedom from anxiety if I am going to be effective, free to do whatever has to be done. There are also some less sensible voices that point out the absurdity of a radical simplification of life-style which will almost certainly mean that I become more dependent on the state and/or my friends, either now or in old age, and thereby consume resources that by right should go to those who really need them. And there is one person on the minibus who insists, seemingly without embarrassment, that there is nothing wrong with a bottle of wine or a decent meal, or a party, or a new overcoat. These things, he insists, with appeals to Old Testament and Rabbinic teaching, are given by God. The enjoyment of them is a way by which we may glorify God.

The row in the minibus is both a recognition of my legion (or our corporate legion) and a beginning of consciousness of our inner essence, our Powers. Which of our legion comes out on top? And why? And where are other members of the party... This line of thinking quickly takes us into depth psychology and into a discussion of the relationship between psychological/spiritual growth and its Christian interpretation. That would take us too far from the main thrust of our argument. Suffice it to say here that exposing the Powers within us to the Person of Christ, in the brokenness of the Cross and in the glory of the Resurrection, is *both* what I take psychological/spiritual growth/healing to be, *and* the reconstitution of consciousness which I have called alternative.[10]

Perhaps it is easier to see at the corporate level. Any collective entity has its own legion. By that I do not mean the tautology that collectives constitute more than one person. Instead I mean that any group of people is likely to be influenced by a number of factors, some conscious (making money, getting re-elected, keeping the PR people happy, doing a good job) and some unconscious. Particular factors will weigh more heavily with some people than with others. Out of this diversity decisions will emerge – or be imposed by a small oligarchy. Either way, the group makes decisions out of a wide, disparate and conflicting body of material. We can ask why such and such a decision was made and however far back we push the explanation there will always be further questions to ask. We can never give a *final* account of why the decision was taken which closes off the possibility of asking again 'But why that . . . ?' For there is finally an unconscious mood, a collective unspoken norm that makes a specific decision come out like this. *There* is the inner essence, the 'power and principality'. And it is that which has to be brought under judgment by being exposed to the paradox of power revealed in the Cross and Resurrection: power that is used for self-aggrandisement is demonic and therefore ultimately self-destructive. Power that is used in accordance with the good news of beatitudes, sermon on the mount and magnificat liberates the powerful from what oppresses them – and in doing so liberates the poor and weak.

We get a glimpse of that in the life and death of Oscar Romero in El Salvador. As Romero tried to live out his own liberation from the power structures of society, Church and state by a close identification with the poor and oppressed through listening to them and sharing with them, he found the contrast between state power, military power and the freedom he was discovering for himself unendurable. 'It is in practice illegal,' he said, 'to be an authentic Christian in our environment. . . precisely because the world around us is founded radically on an established disorder before which the mere proclamation of the gospel is subversive'[11] – words which might well have been used by Desmond Tutu, Allan Boesak or Beyers Naudé in South Africa or even, had they as charismatic a spokesperson, by the poor and oppressed of the global community as they contemplate the use of economic and political power against them.

The liberation of the powerful (and that means, in one sense or another, most people who will read this book) is a theme that has been much neglected in ecumenical debate. One of its most powerful expressions is in William Stringfellow's meditation on Revelation from the perspective of the Vietnam War.

To speak of the Indo-Chinese war in terms of the relation of principalities and human beings is, bluntly, to expose the survival of the Pentagon and its satellites or adjoining principalities as the purpose of the war. . . (That) does not classify America's leaders as nitwits or wicked, though some in fact may be either or both, but discerns their victimisation by the principalities and powers to which they are privy. Their servility to the survival interest of these powers depletes them as human beings. They become captivated, dominated, possessed by the demonic... These relationships between the principalities and human beings, in which human life is sacrificed to sustain the demonic and in which reputed leaders as well as ordinary folk become victims, are more intricate, more complicated, more ambiguous, more tense, more hectic than words can describe. The milieu of the powers and principalities *is* chaos.[12]

The chaotic and demonic nature of the Powers that hold us and our institutions captive imply a need to recognise or identify those Powers at work in those who think they run our institutions. The consciousness that I have called alternative apprehends others – all others, but particularly others who are responsible for institutions and structures – in their trapped-ness, that is to say in the thrall of their Powers. It is worth exploring this, I believe, because without an adequate appreciation of the Powers which hold dominion over others, action of any sort that is designed to be liberating is, in fact, likely to be self-defeating – or worse. We can too easily find ourselves confronting the system rather than the Power behind the system; the minister or the bishop or the tycoon rather than the Powers that hold them (and, God knows, probably us too) in subjection. In other words we have seen so far that we need to become aware of the Powers that act on us: now we acknowledge the need to become aware of the Powers that act on others, individually or collectively.

And it is there that we begin to glimpse, however tentatively, the third, cosmic, level of analysis. For our individual and collective choices – whether they be decisions about production and consumption, about war and peace, or decisions about any other life and death choices – reveal a thread of truth about us and our society that is part of the fabric of the human condition. We behave like this because this is how and what we are. However much we seek to transcend our present limitations, we know we have such limitations. We are back with the Galatians: 'slaves of the ruling spirits', on our way to 'spiritual maturity' (Gal. 4:3). Our individual and collective patterning of expectations, aspirations and activities are related to and influenced by this tension between the rule of 'the spirits' or Powers, and our own journey, through Cross and Resurrection, to spiritual maturity. The choices we make, the way in which we use our freedom, tell us – if we but listen – not only about ourselves, but also about the ultimate realities in which those choices and freedoms are set. And those realities include *both* the 'rule of the spirits' *and* the fact of Christ's victory over that tyrannical, destructive rule.

Now if this account remotely resembles reality, we have three levels of analysis – individual, collective and cosmic – each related to the other. My inner essence is analytically different from, but not existentially wholly separable from, that of my community, my family, my nation. We are related, at our deepest level, dialectically, the one impinging on the other. That dialectic interaction affects and is affected by the great cosmic struggle between the 'spiritual powers' (Gal. 4:3) or the elemental spirits of the Universe (Col. 2:8). We cannot give a precise account of *how* our interaction with the collective order influences and is influenced by the cosmic drama, though we may glimpse it at the extremes of the moral spectrum. The institutionalised violence of the racist state – e.g. in South Africa or Guatemala – and the loving acceptance of redemptive suffering (as explored in Chapter 11) each says something about the interpenetration of historical and cosmic events or energies.

The Pauline literature, moreover, sees the Cross and Resurrection as the two events that most immediately and sharply attest to this interpenetration. It is those events that radically change the realities at all three levels. The cosmic struggle is won, at least in anticipation, and the quality of life ('eternal') is made available to those who seek it so that the consequences of the cosmic victory can now be lived out in the temporal order. The Kingdom of God *can* now come, but it has to be sought, struggled for, constructed.

And that is a task for both the individual and the collective. Or, to put it better, it is a task for the individual-in-the-community. For both poles have to be maintained – the individual and the social – so intense and intimate is the dialectic that holds them together. The task can only be approached, however, in so far as the inner essence of individual and collective are *in fact* redeemed or set free. And they are redeemed, so we believe, by the appropriation of the

Cross and Resurrection; that is, by the willing enablement of redemptive suffering and the Covenant use of power.

Before we turn to that in the next chapter, we have one final topic to explore.

3 Identifying the Powers

So far we have left the Powers somewhat vague. Sure, we have used terms like egocentricity or acquisitiveness or lust to dominate. Those are properly terms that apply to individuals: only by extension, by loose metaphor, do they apply to collectives. Identifying the inner essence of the systems and institutions that impoverish people and nations is, however, a key analytical exercise if we are going to confront them at any level. (I shall turn to the method by which they may be confronted in the next chapter, remaining content to do no more than scatter hints in this chapter.)

This identification of the Powers behind the system is a task that social scientists have long attempted. Indeed, we have already looked at some such attempts. Victims of their age and of their own enthusiasm for a misreading of Marx on materialism, however, they have concentrated on the physical or structural aspects of the elements of the system, while (rightly) dismissing much liberal concern with the effects or working of the system as a vulgar interest in epiphenomena. Wanting to get behind those epiphenomena, those presenting symptoms, they have been content with other material manifestations – e.g. the declining rate of profit to capital – while ignoring the spiritual dimension of the phenomena they have wanted to discuss.

A better approach was that of Marx himself who identified alienation – in at least three senses – both as an inevitable outcome of industrial capitalism and as a deeply-experienced malaise of his contemporary society. For Marx, the capitalist mode of production made the alienation of workers inevitable because it separates the worker not only from nature and the product he produces, but also from 'his spiritual essence, his *human* essence'.

Within the capitalist system all methods for raising the

social productivity of labour are put into effect at the cost of the individual worker... They distort the worker into a fragment of a man, they degrade him to the level of an appendage to a machine... They alienate from him the intellectual potentialities of the labour process in the same proportion as science is incorporated in it as an independent power.[13]

For Marx, this process of alienation results in the worker's alienation from his fellow beings and particularly from those who profit from capitalist production, the owners of capital.

It is not part of my purpose to defend Marxian analysis in general or Marx's theory of alienation in particular. I use it only as an illustration of a way by which we may become more aware of the social processes which embody spiritual Powers that entrap us and those to whom we would relate. One of the unfortunate effects of capitalism is that it does separate and alienate one group of people from another. The storm of protest that greeted Sir Peter Parker's claim, in a speech in December 1985 to the British Institute of Management, that British managers are now less separated from their workers, demonstrated the reality of alienation. It is perhaps doubly significant that the bulk of the protests came from managers themselves, aware of just how deep the process of alienation has gone.

Our difficulty arises because, while it is not too hard for us to apprehend the process that Marx describes within our own workplace or community (and particularly in Britain where class is so deeply-entrenched a feature of our social landscape), it is much more problematic when we try to relate that to the poor of the world. In what possible sense, it might be asked, is a herdsman in Mali or a fisherman in the Philippines alienated from his own human essence by the Powers of global capitalism? Are the spiritual Powers at work the same? And what difference does it make to us? It makes presumably this difference: if I am persuaded that capitalism has at its centre a process that is essentially destructive, I shall be the more cautious about making any choices as consumer, producer, employer, voter, teacher or parent, that threaten alternative economic systems. Those alternative systems may not be efficient in an accountant's sense. They may not even be very robust, in the sense that they can resist neither natural disasters nor inroads from modernisation; but maybe they preserve something essential to the human spirit – a something that capitalism systematically destroys.

If we and some of those to whom we relate are identifiably trapped by the spiritual Powers of alienation, others may be trapped by the spiritual Powers that are embodied in other social processes, including those that are associated with non-capitalist societies. There is indeed an alternative account of alienation itself that locates its origins not in capitalism but in the concentration of power in the Party and bureaucracy and the de-powerment of ordinary people in totalitarian or quasi-totalitarian régimes. No one economic system has a monopoly of alienation: no system is free of Powers that need to be redeemed.

It is not, of course, only economic or politico-economic systems that entrap and enslave people, that become dominated, that is, by demonic Powers which need to be identified, to be known. For example, we might ask, of individuals or communities, if they are integrated or isolated? This is another pole of being human that many would regard as quite as important as levels of consumption. To be isolated, cut off from community, cut off from interaction with others, is as cruel a form of impoverishment and dehumanisation as to be cut off from basic consumption needs. As I struggle for alternative consciousness, then, I need to learn, to apprehend others as social actors, that is as people who may or may not be incorporated into processes of interaction that they find fulfilling.

For example, one criterion by which I might judge a new technology would be its ability to increase human interaction rather than diminish it. This might apply not only to high-tech choices such as interactive television systems, but also to low-tech choices that impinge on the developing world. Anthropological literature is full of examples. The labour migration system in Southern Africa, for instance, has seriously undermined not only family life in households where the men have migrated in search of work, but the life of the whole village and the whole community. The women are left increasingly isolated and many are abandoned by their husbands, who take a common law wife in the town. Because social organisation takes time to catch up with changing circumstances, the women find themselves excluded from community politics in the broadest sense. Having no men to speak for them or represent them in fora in which it is traditional that women do not speak, they find decisions are taken without any possibility of their participation in that process.

The spiritual Powers embodied in this form of social organisation (related, it is worth noting, to a particular form of economic organisation) thus isolate, divide, dis-integrate, make true community impossible. They are, to that extent, demonic and in need of redemption. Alternative consciousness sees people in Southern Africa trapped in that isolation, not only by a particular government but by an array of spiritual Powers which control that government – and the economic and social systems to which it gives rise.

We could take examples from other forms of oppression: from sexism to the militarism already hinted at by String-fellow. I want to finish this chapter and introduce the next by reverting to the cosmic level of analysis. For the spiritual Powers that 'rule' in South Africa or in capitalism-as-a-system or in male chauvinism, can be thought of as manifestations, specific instances, of more general energies that operate at the cosmic level. An analogy, as I have already suggested, is Jung's hypothesis of the collective unconscious, to which the individual unconscious is related and by which it is therefore affected. In much the same way I want to argue that the Powers that hold social entities and structures in (destructive) thrall are related to and affected by Cosmic Powers of generalised destructive energy. We can visualise them as connected by capillaries which conduct their energies in small, discrete doses. In this sense, the Revelation of St John the Divine gives us an account of the cosmic conflict between the life-giving redeeming Powers of Christ (the Lamb) and the Powers of destruction (Babylon). The Lamb is seen as the victor, for at the cosmic level ('eternity' in another biblical code), the life-giving Powers of Christ, incarnated and acted out in Cross and Resurrection, finally triumph over the powers of destruction.

From this it follows that there is, as it were, a parallel between the generalised powers of destruction and their specific instances in structures and individuals on the one hand, and on the other the life-giving Powers of Christ and their embodiment in structures and individuals. Now it is too simplistic (as well as heretical!) to see some structures and individuals as the 'territory' of the former and others the 'territory' of the latter. *We are all the territory of both*, and the struggle for the Kingdom is precisely to reduce the grip of the former and enlarge that of the latter. How may that be done? It is to that which we turn in the next chapter.

Chapter 10

In the last chapter, I argued that the Powers that hold and destroy must be redeemed by being exposed to Christ. We explored this idea with respect to the power to choose as consumers and to see others in their own trappedness. In the course of this exploration, we found that the inward journey, to discover and have redeemed my own Powers, cannot easily be isolated from the outward journey of action in society. I do what I am. If what I am can be liberated from the grip of evil powers that make me so ego-centric, fearful and proud, my actions, whether 'private', social or political will be less damaging to my neighbour – whether that neighbour be in my street or on the far side of the globe. And, so we suggested, if that is true of the individual, it is also true of corporate 'persons'. They, too, must be set free from the demonic powers that grip them, so that they can use power to make actual relationships of a covenant-quality. This freeing is the point at which the cosmic interacts with the personal and the social.

Two questions now remain. How do I *actually* come to terms with my Powers, so that I may be free of whatever is demonic in them? And how do institutions *actually* secure release from the demonic powers that make them impoverish the poor and oppress the weak?

On the first question I have only a little to add to the vast and wide-ranging literature on conversion and sanctification or, to use a language with which I personally am more comfortable, spiritual healing. What little I do have to add I dare to contribute from within the context of the focus of this particular book. I want to make four points, and in the process touch on some parts of the second question.

1 The Call

First, most works on spiritual healing emphasise that the

initiative is God's: he 'calls' us out of our comfortable, selfish rut into a new, often turbulent process of growth. In that context, it seems to me that one way in which that call is often mediated is the exposure to the raw need of others. By this I emphatically do not mean to imply that an emotional response to televised pictures of starving people in Ethiopia, for example, is (or is *necessarily*) the way in which the call to the inward journey of alternative consciousness is heard. Nor even is a commitment to the outward journey – 'This must be changed' – to be confused with the consciousness of the gentle drawing forward into a deeper relationship with God. Rather, I suspect the exposure to the raw need of others can sometimes illuminate with a new kind of light, the nature, the ontological quality, of Christ's own suffering. Let me illustrate.

A young Church executive was, as he imagined, very busy about his Father's business. Assiduously he hurried from meeting to meeting, hopping on planes as other people hop on buses, and co-ordinating a great ecumenical effort that would surely usher in the Kingdom of God. One evening his pressured life of ecumenical activity took him to the unlikely location of Ankara, the capital of Muslim Turkey. He was booked into a large modern hotel and apart from a short-lived frisson of discomfort at the contrast between his environment and the nature of his work, he settled down to enjoy his stay. After an excellent dinner he went for a short walk through the market quarter of Ankara.

On his way, he saw two urchins crouched in a doorway, their clothes in tatters, no shoes on their feet. Both were thin and shivering, one was in tears. He walked on back to the comfort of his hotel room. He prepared for bed and began the evening office. He had barely opened his prayerbook when the full horror of his position seized him.

He dressed quickly, ran through the streets – back to the doorway where he had seen the two youths. They had gone. For the next two hours, he combed the streets looking for them. He failed to find them. He went back to his room and wept the bitter tears of self-knowledge the rest of the night. He had heard the call to the inward journey of alternative consciousness in that anguish. Although he knows he is forgiven and accepted, the resonance of that anguish lives with him still.

My critics will object that while it may make sense to talk of exposure to the raw needs of others as one way whereby the call to the inward journey may be heard, that is essentially an individual matter. Does it make any sense in a corporate dimension? I believe so. Surely the experience of many religious Orders, dioceses, and even the Bishops' Conference of Latin America at both Medellin and Puebla is precisely that the Church as a corporate being can hear the call to conversion through exposure to the need of the poor and the powerless. Although there was of course more to it than that (for example, the whole ecclesiological and theological ferment leading up to and following from Vatican II) it would be hard to deny that the process of sharing with the poor, particularly in Brazil and Central America which began with Medellin, had a profound effect in shifting the perspective of the Catholic Church in Latin America. It shifted it from a charitable concern to ease the suffering of the poor to a determination to change the structural position of the poor – and in the process to subject the institutional Church both to a radical social critique and, more significantly from our present standpoint, a deepening spirituality that would sustain the Church in that process.

Although the Latin American experience is perhaps the most striking and the best documented, it is not unique. The Church in South Korea has developed a whole new way of understanding both the nature of the Church and the nature of the Faith, through seeing the suffering of people who in the name of Christ were prepared to confront the power structures of a repressive anti-poor régime. Minjung theology is, of course, still in the process of discovery, but it has already changed radically both the self-understanding of the Church and its understanding of the nature of the inward journey.[1]

We need, however, to be careful. For it seems that exposure to the raw needs of the poor and the powerless enables some parts of the Church to hear the call to a new inward journey to alternative consciousness, while others find it impossible to hear that call. Thus when we talk of the Church in Latin America responding to Medellin and Puebla, and hearing in the experiences reflected there the call to the inward journey to alternative consciousness, we have to recognise that that process split the Church – split it far more fundamentally than the historical lines of division between, for example, Catholic and Episcopalian or Episcopalian and Methodist. In a rather less dramatic way the Anglican Church's work on inner city deprivation was condemned as 'Marxist' by those people who regard themselves as 'good C of E'.

That itself is, of course, neither surprising nor inconsistent with the biblical record: the Word of God divides and judges. Theologically and institutionally, however, we find that fact hard to cope with. In South Africa, for instance, the celebrated Kairos document, calling on Christians individually and the Churches corporately to see the struggle of black South Africans to be free of racism and apartheid as part of the liberating activity of Almighty God himself, both reflects and maintains a deep division within all the mainline Churches.[2] Some see the document as the inscription of the call itself. Perhaps in choosing that title the authors do themselves. Others see it as dangerous political propaganda which will stir up opposition, dissension and persecution, making reconciliation all the more difficult. Such a division of opinion is exactly what one would expect – and exactly what Western Churches typically find it so hard to come to terms with.

2 Hearing the Call

This brings me to my second point. If *one* way in which God's initiative in spiritual healing is mediated is through exposure to the raw needs of others, we need to ask how that 'call' may be heard. Or, to put the same question in a language we have already used, how is the call to the inward journey to alternative consciousness heard? Along with Martin Israel and a long tradition of mystical writers, I suggest that exposure to one's own poverty through the experience of suffering is very often a way in which the call to the inward journey is most insistently presented.[3]

At the individual level that suffering may be physical – through illness, unemployment, sudden impoverishment, homelessness, persecution or the deprivation of liberty. Father Gerry Hughes, the well-known Jesuit who works with the Peace Movement in the United Kingdom and Ireland, has commented how people who have suddenly suffered for their moral and political convictions about peace and/or disarmament have changed.

'There is just something different about them,' says Father Hughes. 'Once they have been roughed up by the police, or put in the police cells, or had a summary trial and been put in prison, even if only for a week, it's almost as though a light comes on, a light deep down in their innermost selves. It's no longer their outward superficial selves that are engaged. They are now engaged at a far deeper level and they experience a thirst, almost a terrible thirst, for sustenance at the level.'

I do not want to be misunderstood. I am not saying that all suffering is good, or even that good can be brought out of all suffering. Nor am I saying that personal suffering is a necessary condition of the inward journey to alternative consciousness. Indeed, it is neither a necessary nor a sufficient condition of that journey. Particularly in contrast to those whom Martin Marty calls 'summer Christians',[4] I am anxious to re-state an observation that has long been part of the Christian tradition, namely that the discovery of one's own inner poverty through suffering is one way, perhaps a neglected way, in which the call to the inward journey (and for that matter the outward journey too) can become real.

Again we need to ask whether this is purely an individual condition or whether it is something that can be experienced corporately. Specifically, can the Church discover the inner dynamic to alternative consciousness through suffering? Many of the cases that we looked at in the last paragraphs could be called in evidence again. However, we need to be aware that there are counter-examples, examples, that is, of great suffering by the Church in persecution, resulting less in a call to alternative consciousness than a kind of involution, a desperate clinging to dogma, patterns of authority, liturgical convention – not because they give life or liberty, but because they represent forms of security that the persecuted come, understandably, to value highly. Visitors to China, for example, often comment on the conservative nature – theologically, liturgically, ecclesiastically – of the Church in China.

3 The Desert Experience

Third, and consistent with both the former points, it is worth repeating that the call to alternative consciousness can be experienced as a call to the desert. It is worth emphasising that in this context, since liberation theology is sometimes misread to be assurance that liberation is an easy, quick, costless or delightful experience. Western readers of popularised versions of some of the great minds of liberation theology can be given the idea that once we identify with the poor and live in solidarity with them, our liberation – in the sense of our freedom from our own demonic powers – will be instantaneous and complete. We shall, so it might be assumed, live holy, happy, well-integrated lives, secure from spiritual corruption. That making that leap of solidarity *is* a major liberation I do not deny: the empirical evidence is overpowering for any open-minded visitor to Central America or north-east Brazil. We need to remember, however, that a longer tradition warns us of the reality of the desert experience for those who embark on this journey.

For the testimony of the mystics and saints over the centuries is that the inward journey is nearly always a journey to the desert. It is a calling out from a settled life of comfort and ease and security and a symbolic surrender to a new kind of living. 'The land to which God has brought you is not like the land of Egypt from which you came out. You can no longer live here as you lived there. Your old life and your former self are crucified now and you must not seek to live any more for your own gratification... Above all (you must) eat your daily bread; without it you cannot live...'[6]

The leaving of Egypt does not guarantee entry into the Promised Land of rootedness. On the contrary. Once the Israelites left the security of their homes in Egypt, they were literally bewildered in a country which was for them entirely and sometimes terrifyingly new. No wonder they objected. No wonder they berated Moses for giving them a freedom and an opportunity that they would rather not have taken. 'Weren't there any graves in Egypt? Did you have to bring us out here to die? It would be better to be slaves there than to die here in the desert' (Exod. 14:10–12).

At the core of the desert experience lies fear. In the religious consciousness of Israel the fear of the desert is directly linked to idolatry. Fear drives us to ascribe worth, and finally ultimate worth, to false gods, false values – as Stringfellow reminded us in the last chapter. We fear that Almighty God will leave us to perish in the desert and so we look around desperately for false saviours. We become adept at dressing up our false saviours in religious clothing – the institutional church, doctrinal orthodoxy, liturgical practice, or even raising money for charity. These religious substitutes seem to offer us a certitude, a security, an immediacy, that delivers us from the vague wanderings, the apathy and anomie of the desert. We invest our all in them in order to be delivered from the fear of desolation in the desert.

The lust for false security in the desert is, of course, the visible symptom of a fundamental lack of trust. And that is the paradox. It is in the nature of the desert that we feel lost in it, overpowered by it: we feel lonely and afraid. *That is* the desert.

Fear is not, however, limited to the desert. Even when we have passed through the desert, we are dogged by fear. As we review our outward journey from the perspective of the inward journey, we are struck by the immensity of the powers or Powers with which the outward journey brings us into conflict. The powers of the state, the powers of the Church, the powers of greed and self-interest, of fear, of apathy, of convention, of good manners – all the powers seem ranged against us and we quake. But fear is not confined to the outward journey: in a way even more fearsome is the acknowledgement of self-destruction of the legion we encounter in our deepest selves on our inward journey. We have already mentioned the people in the minibus and seen how easily they bicker amongst themselves, argue, fight, oppress and repress each other so that the progress of the minibus itself is put in jeopardy.

One measure both of the universality of fear and of its destructive potential is the frequency with which the people of God, in both Old Testament and New, are urged not to give way to fear. In nearly every religious tradition represented in the Old Testament, from the two great schools of historians to the Psalmist, the eighth-century prophets and the prophets of the Restoration, the common theme is the call to supersede fear with trust. The New Testament inherits and re-emphasises the same elemental point of religious consciousness.

It is often said that throughout the Bible appearances of God or angels are attended by the encouragement not to be frightened. That is true, but it is only a part of the truth. The wider truth is that the deeper the awareness of God's activity in securing salvation for His people, the more central the fear/trust tension is presented. To take one example of many, consider the legend of Peter walking on the water. Here we have a story that can be read at many levels, but at whatever level we take it, we have to do justice to the symbolism of stormy water, the boat, Christ's previous period of prayer, and Peter's failure. A possible reconstruction of those symbols is the contrast between the trust that is deeply rooted in prior meditation – the inward journey – and the fear that overwhelms Peter as he is challenged to move from the security of the known into the insecurity of the deeper consciousness.

Yet there is more here. For, paradoxically, it is a consciousness of weakness, a recognition of ultimate dependence on God, which makes possible God's salvific action. Grace and weakness are umbilically related: Grace is not only made perfect in weakness (2 Cor. 12:9). Weakness is a precondition of grace being effective. The non-fearful recognition of weakness, of lostness, of ultimate dependence upon the certainty of God's love, thus lies at the heart of the inward journey.

Can any of this make sense with respect to structures? After all, if we talk of structural sin, should we not also, like Father Tom Cullinan, talk of structural grace?[7] And if we talk of structural grace, then the logic of the last paragraph suggests that we have to talk of structures being non-fearfully aware of weakness, of lostness, of dependence. Does this make any sense? Can, indeed, any structure, any institution undertake this part of the inward journey?

Once again I think the question has to be asked and answered primarily of the institutional church. It does not seem fanciful to suggest that a Church, the Church, can experience fear in the three senses we have already discussed: fear of the desert, fear of the external powers, and fear of the powers of internal disintegration.

Whether one looks at the Church in the United States during the Civil Rights Movement and the Vietnam War protest; or whether one looks at the Church in South Africa facing apartheid; or at the Church in the United Kingdom facing radical Thatcherism, one can detect a series of pathologies of fear. Around each cluster of issues, fear is generated that the Church *as an institution* might be being called into the terrible desert of lonely witness, shorn of the false securities of respectability, political and social acceptability, and financial security. Notice the reaction of most Anglican Churchmen to talk of disestablishment of the Church of England. Similarly, there is fear of what 'they' will do to us: that is to say, fear that the external powers will somehow wreak vengeance on the institutional Church. They did precisely that, after all, in the Southern United States, during the height of the Civil Rights movement, to many individual Christians and individual congregations who identified themselves as supporters of civil rights. In very different terms, less violently but more invidiously, the powers took vengeance on the progressive Church leadership of the National Council of Churches of the USA in 1982–83 for being 'soft on communism', that is, supporting the struggle of poor people in many parts of the world including Nicaragua, Mozambique, Cuba and Vietnam.

The powers of this world do hit back: they hit back hard and they hit to hurt. The Church is right in appreciating that this is not a phoney war; it's not a pillow-fight. There is plenty to be frightened about. The question is whether the Church as an institution is then so dominated by that fear that it ceases to trust in the grace of the Lord who promises that He will never desert it.

The fear of inner disintegration, the legion fear, haunts any voluntary association of free individuals. The Church's history of schism, division and, less visible but much more common, disenchanted members voting with their feet and leaving the Church altogether, is again ground for real fear. Of course the Church can fall to pieces. Of course it can lose membership. The fear is real and the Church is not guaranteed deliverance from that reality, any more than it is guaranteed deliverance from vengeance by the external powers or the inward terror of the desert. Of course not. The question, however, remains the same: is the fear of internal disintegration allowed to dictate the terms of the inward journey, or is it seen as an invitation to yet deeper trust in the hope of more abundant grace?

4 Encouragement from the Bottom

This brings me to the fourth and final point I want to make as a kind of extended footnote to the literature on conversion, spiritual growth and healing. The terror of the desert and of the fears I have just been describing are real enough at both the individual and institutional levels. Paradoxically perhaps, the lesson of Central America, South Africa, South Korea and the Philippines is that we, the affluent comfortable Christians of the North, can derive encouragement from those who have more to fear than we shall ever conceive. I am aware of the danger of sounding romantic at this point and for that very reason I shall resist telling stories of courage, endurance and resistance with which each of those regions abounds. Instead, I want to make a more general point. Part of the process of growth in alternative consciousness is learning to receive – and especially receive from people seemingly less well provided than us. Partly because we so completely misunderstand the parable of the Good Samaritan (which is, in fact, about receiving rather than about giving) and partly because it flatters our vanity, it has become part of our cultural heritage to imagine that the *only* response to others whom we perceive as less fortunate than ourselves is to give of our abundance.

We shall never learn to give until we learn to receive; and most of us find that a far harder lesson. When we receive the testimony of people who have journeyed far in alternative consciousness and faced the consequences – and they are usually little people at the bottom of the stack – we are beginning to make that leap of consciousness which enabled the orthodox Jew to receive help from the unclean, deeply despised Samaritan. In the darkest parts of our fears – both the inner fears and the outer threats – we can receive from peasants in Central America, sugar cane cutters in the Philippines and unemployed, illicit settlers in the black townships of South Africa an assurance that God is greater than our fears. For many such people have tested that assurance to the limits of their own lives. If we would but hear them, give them space and opportunity, they can tell us all we need to know about grace being made perfect in weakness. As long as we respond to their reality only – or even at all – by bombarding them with modernisation projects, we shall not enable them to share their richness with us. We rob ourselves – but in the process we rob them of the dignity of giving.

5 Facing the Institutional Powers

Finally I turn to the less traditional question of how institutions and systems may be freed from the demonic Powers that hold them captive. What does it mean to 'show Christ' to them (Eph. 3:10)? It is worth emphasising at the outset that, if we are to be faithful to a New Testament understanding of power, it is Christ that redeems our structures. We need to grasp that, in order to be delivered from the conventional notion that it is *we* who redeem them – from either within or from without. That is the absurdity of much contemporary politics, either mainstream or 'alternative'. It legitimates a return to crude power-plays where brute force, low cunning or full coffers (and preferably all three) are the final arbiters of history.

As long as our structures are in the grip of demonic powers, the stuff of our politics, the way power is acquired and used, will be as crude as that. And the notion that by manipulating the same levers we can transform the nature of those politics is simply false – as false, almost literally, as the notion that we can haul ourselves up (physically or morally) by our own boot-straps. That is not to deny that some policies and some politicians are more evil than others; or to imply that there is nothing to choose between Ferdinand Marcos or Cory Aquino; or between the Strategic Defence Initiative and nuclear disarmament. By no means. But it is to insist that the powers of corruption, of moral disintegration, of undisguised evil have to be overcome in the essence of our structures if we are to begin to see in our institutions the possibility of covenant-quality relationships. Too much of our time and energy is focused on the surface-film of politics: what we have to penetrate, or rather what we have to allow Christ to penetrate, is the moral substratum of the way power is acquired and used. How may that awesome task be done?

A preliminary point needs to be made. There is a long Christian tradition, maintained by some great masters of spirituality today, that assumes that if *individuals* (that is the 'key' individuals) can begin the journey to alternative consciousness, then the institutions they control will be redeemed. 'Convert the right people and the structures will convert themselves.' That has been the missionary strategy of most mainline Churches in the North for centuries: how else explain the scramble to found (and keep in being) denominational schools and colleges for the super-privileged, or the targetting of so many resources on the centres of power, either actual or potential, for example, the leafy suburbs and the smarter universities? We have simply assumed that élites *control* the structures they come to head.

That is not, as I have already argued, the view of the New Testament. It is decreasingly the view of organisational sociologists. And it is not the experience of many of the more reflective institutional leaders who, often to their chagrin, discover that when they finally struggle to the top of their particular tree, their capacity to influence events, even within their own organisation, is little more than marginal. (Thus Harold Macmillan, reflecting on his years as prime minister: 'You strive to get to the top and when you get there, what do you find? Dust...') We have to return, then, to the basic position that it is the demonic powers that control structures and organisations. It is those powers that have to be confronted and overcome if the structures are to be set free. How?

It is as well to start by acknowledging that we are dealing with mystery, with the deepest workings of the redemptive power of Christ. Accordingly I have no slick formula, no ready answers – any more than I have for the seeming randomness of why A is enabled and sustained in the process of conversion and growth in alternative consciousness, while B, perhaps to her own chagrin, remains stuck at the beginning of the beginning of that journey. There do seem, nonetheless, to be a number of pointers, straws in the wind, that are worth sharing.

In the last chapter I spoke of experiencing others in their trappedness, whether the others be individuals or structures. Very often, however, the other is not aware of that trappedness: they imagine they are free. One of the greatest ironies, I would even say tragedies, of the situation in Southern Africa today is that the Nationalist Government sees itself as defending 'freedom' against 'tyranny', while conscripting young men into the armed forces, spending a high proportion of national income on the forces of internal repression and arming the white civilian population to defend itself against riot. That is an easy example of false consciousness, to steal a term from another (but not unrelated) debate. More difficulties are posed by some of the economic structures we reviewed earlier. In what sense, for example, are international commodity traders aware of their own trappedness in a structure of systemic injustice? They will say that without the market they provide, the developing world would be worse off. They will argue that the market must be enabled to function smoothly, to adapt to shocks and disturbances, to keep producers in touch with the needs of consumers. They see their role as entirely beneficial, or perhaps as morally neutral. And there is a sense in which they are right. For what is demonic is the system, not (or not necessarily) the individuals who operate the system.

In much the same way, the international monetary system, currently draining Africa of over thirty per cent of the value of its exports to service its debts, at a time when reconstruction and recovery requires huge inflows of capital[8], is a demonic structure for which it is difficult to identify particular individuals as personally responsible. Responsibility is so diffused through the Treasuries and Finance Ministries of the US, Germany, Japan and the EEC that the whole idea of personal responsibility – and therefore personal power – becomes inoperable. Certainly one can identify a dozen key actors, but in no sense are they free agents, by whose fiat the whole structure could be changed. Those individuals and the bureaucracies and power-systems they represent are trapped, not only in the sense that they cannot change the system, but in the deeper sense that they are ideologically blinded to the fact that it needs to be changed. For they are caught in a web of value systems and explanations that 'justify' the present arrangements by which Africa is systematically impoverished – and all for the sake of her own poor!

Our first question therefore has to be this: how can trapped structures be confronted with the consequences of their own existence? As C. S. Song has pointed out in his important study *Third Eye Theology*,[9] the gospels give us some good examples of precisely this process. Song shows, for example, that many of Jesus's parables are to be seen as indirect ways of calling to account those who maintain oppressive structures, reminding them of the need to judge those structures from the standpoint of those who are oppressed rather than from that of those who benefit.[8] For example, Song reminds us that in the parable of the workers in the vineyard, Jesus is using material that would instantly be recognised by his audience as originating in the Song of the Vineyard in Isaiah 5. So far from being a story about (or *only* about) the coming of the Messiah to judge the wicked tenants, this context makes it clear that it is a story that spells out the core of Jesus's Kingdom teaching – that the time is ripe for the evil powers of economic and political structures to be transformed. For the Song of the Vineyard finishes with a word of judgment: 'He looked for justice and found it denied: for righteousness but heard cries of distress'. Parabolically, Jesus is demanding justice and right-dealing for the contemporary victims of injustice – as the hallmark of the inbreaking of the Messiah, the start of the Kingdom of God.

Another example is the parable of the talents, much used, incidentally, to laud the values of aggressive capitalism. Song reads the parable in exactly the opposite sense. For him, the central point of the parable is that the non-entrepreneurial servant, who hid his talent in the ground, becomes the accuser of the king. The king demands high economic performance and rewards those who achieve it. But the third servant, far from cowering in self-disgust at his poor rate of return, rounds on the king and shows him to be unjust, unreasonable and avaricious. He reaps other men's fields; gathers other men's crops. He is a thief in courtly garb. . . . And Jesus tells the story in language that would again strike Old Testament resonances with his audience. This time the reference is to Exodus, the classic tale, re-enacted every Passover, of liberation from oppression and systemic injustice.

Jesus is thus constantly pleading for a recognition by those in authority of the demands of the Covenant – that their power and influence be used for the greatest good of the marginal and the excluded. He does so, however, in full recognition of the ultimate source of power and the need for the structures of power to be transformed. We see the clearest statement of that in St John's account of his trial. There is Jesus, beaten, manacled, utterly humiliated before the very essence of the Roman Imperium, literally on trial for his life. Yet he takes charge of the dialogue, contrasting the nature of his kingdom with the nature of Pilate's power. Jesus's kingdom is one in which the spiritual powers of darkness are judged for their destructive effects on the Son of Man and those with whom he surrounds himself. Pilate's use of his authority reflects precisely those powers of darkness – not least because he fails to recognise its true origins.

Here we have, I believe, a vital clue to the question of how we begin to open the structures of injustice to the redeeming love of Christ. We have to confront them, not in a spirit of condemnation and anger – which would itself merely reveal how little progress we had made on our own inward journey – but in a way that achieves the following objectives:

a) reveals the effects of those structures on the poor and vulnerable: 'I looked for justice and found...'

b) places us alongside those who suffer those effects: it is a real confrontation, not a cosy chat between those in collusion.

c) raises questions about the system, the structure (the powers in the language we have borrowed from Wink), rather than about its agents.

d) looks for total transformation, not ameliorative reform: 'I came into the world for this: to bear witness to the truth,' (John 18:37).

e) accepts that the consequences of such a challenge will often be unpleasant, and can include death, possibly at the hands of the religious establishment. (That may seem melodramatic in UK and US. It seems a lot less so in Central America, South Africa and South Korea, exactly those countries from which, I have already suggested, we have much to learn.)

f) accepts that the process of confrontation *does not*, of itself, transform structures. It may challenge them, educate them, shock them into a deeper awareness of what their essence looks like from the bottom. In the end, however, transformation is the work of the Spirit.

g) sees, therefore, the process of structural transformation as a gift, a gift we all, both individually and corporately, need to share. For we are all engaged on the same (or perhaps a similar) journey.

Again we need to ask about the cash value of such criteria. Are we dealing in utopian dreams – or can we find examples of Christians confronting the powers in ways consistent with these seven points?

Chapter 11

The question raised at the end of the last chapter is a fair one –
and one that demands an answer if our discussion is to be
rooted in the real experience of real people. We need models
which show us how the powers behind institution and
structures may be confronted and 'shown Christ'. Perhaps
surprisingly, it seems to me that there is no shortage of such
models. Let us leave aside those associated with one
charismatic figure – Martin Luther King, Dorothy Day,
Mahatma Gandhi, Helder Camara, Vinobha Bhave – not
because they are not relevant or important, but because it
might be argued that what happened around them was
crucially and casually linked to their own charisma. Instead, I
want to look at four examples which do not depend upon
charismatic individuals, but which might nonetheless be
thought to meet the seven criteria I listed at the end of Chapter
10.

1 Witness for Peace

First, the Witness for Peace in Nicaragua seems to me an
almost classic example of the Gospel in action. Briefly, the
Witness started as a result of a tour of the war zone on the
Honduras-Nicaragua border by a group of American Christians who wanted to gain first-hand knowledge about the
conflict in that area. They lived with the people in the villages
along the border and heard their stories. Though by no means
all would identify with the aims and ideological load of the
Sandinista government, all were struck by the constant
assertions of the people that they were less frightened, more

able to criticise and take part in local decision-making and less impoverished under the Sandinistas than they had been under Somoza. Their major complaint, however, was constant harassment and intimidation by the so-called Contras, many of whom had been members of the dreaded National Guard under Somoza.

The American Christians were told that the military activities of the Contras declined in the areas where they, the Americans, were known to be staying, because the Contras knew that if an American was killed, the US government would be unable to continue to support them.

From that observation sprang the idea in 1982 of a permanent American (and, later, international) presence along the border, wherever the fighting or threat of fighting was most pronounced. Groups of American citizens, from particular localities, covenanted with each other and the whole Witness to prepare spiritually for their stay on the border, to learn methods of non-violent resistance, to share the lives of the villagers while they were on the border, and to tell their stories to whoever would listen (and especially to legislators) on their return.

Each group was (is) commissioned at an ecumenical gathering of all the Churches from the area concerned. Such commissionings are deeply moving experiences for those leaving for Nicaragua and those in whose name they depart. There can be no doubt in the minds of those involved that the powers of evil are to be confronted, not in a spirit of hatred or personal condemnation, but in the Spirit of Christ, that longs for reconciliation on the basis of justice and the end of oppression of the poor – in a word, *Shalom*. It is exactly that spirit that informs the political and educational work of the returning Witnesses, as they give evidence to Congressional committees, media conferences and church groups in their own locality – a process in which they derive support from each other. And it is in that spirit that thousands of people, not all of them returned Witnesses, have pledged to take to the streets in passive resistance should the United States decide to invade Nicaragua.

It would be helpful if I could produce concrete evidence that the Witness for Peace has exposed to the light of Christ the demonic powers of the State Department and the Pentagon.

That I cannot do. What is clear, however, is that the 'military option' which commanded very widespread support in the Administration and much (though not all) of the Republican party in Congress in 1983–84 (and which perhaps reached its zenith with the invasion of Grenada) has gradually receded into the background. This is not to claim that US policy has become more tolerant; even less that the (temporary?) abandonment of invasion plans is solely the result of the Witness for Peace. It may not be wholly without significance, however, that attacks on the Witness from the Administration and its influential allies coincided with an apparent back-off from a military confrontation. Coincidence? Possibly. We are never given certainty in such matters: and it is wise to avoid the lust for visible success. Indeed, my other examples have no success after which to lust!

2 Peace Movement

My second model is the peace movement in the United Kingdom. (It has close relations in the US and in other European countries. I confine myself to the United Kingdom only for the sake of focus, and because I am better acquainted with it.) The 'peace movement' is not, of course, a monolithic structure – a feature that is one of its strengths. Rather than describe any or all of its components – many of which are likely to be well known to readers of this book – it might be more useful to consider the seven criteria above from the standpoint of the major components of the peace movement: the Campaign for Nuclear Disarmament, Christian CND, Pax Christi.

How far does the peace movement reveal the effects of reliance on nuclear weapons, and particularly first strike capability, on the poor and the vulnerable? In one sense, this is the most basic point of all in the whole campaign – that *no one* can expect to survive nuclear war. We are all vulnerable, and in so far as the nuclear arms race makes more rather than less likely the eventual use of nuclear arms (and it is that point which is still the most contentious), the possession of nuclear arms makes the whole of the developed world vulnerable. It is also the case that the peace movement has recently, particularly following the work of Ruth Sigard, Richard Jolly and Willy Brandt, put more emphasis on the economic cost of nuclear deterrence in particular, and excessive arms expenditure in general.[1] This line of thinking is complex and uncertain, partly because non-nuclear defence is almost certainly more expensive than nuclear; and partly because there is no guarantee that money saved on defence would be spent in ways that are socially more constructive. Moreover the link between excessive (nuclear and/or conventional) armaments in the North is related only weakly and indirectly to excessive expenditure on armaments in the South. If spending on arms in the North were cut by thirty per cent, would the major arms importers in the Third World significantly reduce their purchases?

This takes us into the substance of a difficult debate, and that is not my purpose here. Instead, I want to argue that the peace movement as a model of confronting the powers does indeed reveal the effects of nuclear arms on the vulnerable; that it is increasingly raising wider questions about the misuse of scarce resources in pursuing technologies of destruction (questions raised to a higher power, of course, by the Strategic Defence Initiative); and that it is making connections (sometimes, as I have hinted, over-simplified connections) between arms expenditures in the North and resource-scarcity in the South.

Is the peace movement one of genuine solidarity with the victims or of persuasion and consultation with the authorities – with all the dangers of manipulation and co-option that the latter bring? The record of the movement surely speaks for itself – from the women's camp at Greenham Common to Peace Eucharists at Faslane and Molesworth. We are not dealing here with a mild protest from within the bosom of the Establishment – a mode of operation so much preferred by Churches established in law or in mentality – but with a popular movement that incorporates (in the full, literal sense of that word) people from every walk of life who see themselves as representing – I would almost say incarnating – the whole of humanity that is threatened by destruction.

'I am not here just for my grandchildren,' a septuagenarian grande-dame once said to me as she sat at the feet of two policemen who were preparing to carry her into the police van.

'I am here for the grandchildren you haven't even thought about yet, and then for the grandchildren of kids in India or Tokyo. I am even here,' she added, with a twinkle and a jerk of her thumb over her shoulder, 'for *their* great grandchildren – not, I suppose, that that will make them any gentler.'

The third criterion is in some ways the most central: does the peace movement raise questions about the structure of defence? At its best, it raises questions about an even more basic issue – the nature and origins of security itself. Christians within the peace movement often raise that question in theological terms: is there not something idolatrous, they ask, about *defining* security in terms of relative destructive power? If we believe in a God who acts in history to redeem his people and draw them to his Kingdom, is not the equation of 'security' with increasing power to destroy (and many students of probability theory would now say likelihood of destroying) the whole globe itself demonic? This line of argument becomes all the more acute as it becomes clear that NATO strategy is based on first-strike capability; and SDI strategy is based on the permanent destabilisation of the balance of terror.

The fourth criterion was a search for total transformation, rather than ameliorative reform. The peace movement splinters along this spectrum. There are some who want a freeze on further production of nuclear weapons, followed by a gradual de-escalation of stocks until all nuclear weapons are destroyed. This is sometimes seen as the most 'politically realistic' option: and so it may prove. The power language of the Bible, however, seems to speak more radically than that: it seems to demand the redemption not only of defence strategies, but of that means of aggression and defensiveness that makes defence strategies 'necessary'. Transformation is not about the choice of weapon systems: it is about choices of how we live in a community of nations, how we view others, how we deal with our individual and corporate projections, so that we see 'them' not as something to be loathed, feared and resisted, but rather as something to be befriended, integrated and neutralised (which is not the same as accepting their ideology or way of life). The women at Greenham Common have sometimes expressed this by the use of powerful symbols of the absurd – attaching dolls and teddy bears to the perimeter fence, throwing streamers and balloons at the missile launchers, standing in silence with lighted candles before the riot police. The clown is a long-hallowed Christian symbol of revolutionary transformation, because he reveals the absurdity of the accepted norms of behaviour. The women have been clowns, committed to a degree and level of transformation that mocks the powers of evil.

Such clowning inevitably invites retribution from the powers. The peace people have received it. From physical violence, perverted justice, and ecclesiastical harassment to acts of crude vandalism (e.g. the Greenham women having their eating utensils smeared with dog-shit), those who contest idolatries of security have paid, and continue to pay, the price.

The penultimate criterion is more difficult to assess. No doubt many in the peace movement do believe that, in time and with increased public support, their protest will achieve the nature of transformation I discussed above. Some, however, know that as long as the debate is left at the level of public support, the crude mathematics of so-called democracy, what is achieved is no more than a change in public policy rather than a transposition of the nature of the debate, and the values and assumptions that underlie it. It is for that reason, perhaps, that many of those most actively involved in the peace movement find, sometimes to their own great surprise having been 'out of the Church' for a long time, that they begin to experience a longing for spiritual sustenance at a depth that far transcends the head-dominated argumentativeness of the politicians. Their outward journey of confrontation of the powers of evil has opened to them the demands of the inward journey to new depths in themselves.

It is that discovery that brings us to the last criterion. It is the discovery of the parallels between the inward journey and the outward journey that brings many of the peace people to a realisation of the giftedness of transformation. It is a gift to be received – and its reception involves letting go of whatever clutters up our individual and corporate capacity to receive. Only empty hands can receive a gift. Being ready to wait with empty hands is near the heart of the spiritual journey.

In this whole discussion it is important not to romanticise. The peace movement, like the Church, is a human institution, the familiar mix of infinite fallibility and glory. It contains people who come from very different directions; have travelled different roads at different speeds in different postures. If what I have described sounds over-idealised, I plead in extenuation that it is a realistic description of the heart, the essence, of many people who have become involved in confronting the powers of nuclear destruction. That even the most reflective and mature are still human beings who, in common with the rest of us, fall far short of the glory to which they are called merely serves to underline the wonder of what together, as a community, they have seen and suffered. After all, the inward and outward journeys are related dialectically. If we all had to wait until we had completed the inward journey before we began the outward journey, the demonic powers would be well pleased – not least because we would never, in fact, make much headway in the inward journey itself.

3 Christian Institute of Southern Africa

My third example of confronting the powers is a clear failure – at least in the instant judgment of contemporary reportage. The Christian Institute in South Africa was founded in 1963 and banned in 1977. In its short life, it attempted to confront the powers in the Dutch Reformed Church, whence came its original leadership and inspiration and, having despaired of that, in the South African state at large. Throughout its existence, however, an important secondary objective was to remind the whole Church of God in South Africa 'that the apartheid ideology cannot be squared with the Gospel of Jesus Christ'.[2] The powers that the CI was confronting were therefore of three orders – the State as an institution, an ideology as the motive force of that state, and the Churches as the people of God, who had to choose between compromising with an ideology that is inherently evil or confessing Christ in their everyday, work-place lives and paying the price.

There is little point in repeating the history of the CI here, for a number of accounts of its life and death are already in print. In brief outline, the story can be told in terms of a gradual approach to the seven criteria I have already described, especially those of solidarity, the rejection of reformism, the acceptance of persecution and the recognition of the giftedness of transformation. For in its inception the CI was intended as a ginger-group within the Nederduitse Gereformeed Kerk, the more conservative sister church, the Nederduitsch Hervormde Kerk, having disassociated itself from any condemnation of racism from the outset. The group of ministers and lay people within the NGK who wanted to change its policies and orientation was, however, always small – and always under attack as communist-sympathisers, heretics and dangers to Church, state and Volk. That suspicion deepended as the CI branched out from an attempt, using study groups, publications, conferences and training programmes, at influencing the NGK to a broader agenda. This change was first signalled by the issuing, in association with the South African Council of Churches, *The Message to the People of South Africa* and then the establishment of the Study Project on Christianity in Apartheid Society, known universally as Spro-Cas. Spro-Cas 'was a response to the question: what does *The Message* actually mean in terms of education, law, economics, the Church, politics and society as a whole? It is one thing for the Church to be prophetic, it is another for it to provide concrete models and alternatives to apartheid, as well as strategies for change, which take into account the complex realities of the South African situation'.[3] The demonic powers of the social systems of apartheid were to be confronted, but still at the intellectual level.

By 1970, the domination by white liberals of CI, Spro-Cas and the work sparked off by *The Message* was coming under challenge, especially from blacks affected by the black consciousness movement. For the CI this was a critical time. Should it retreat in the face of the challenge of black consciousness, to continue its intellectual work in theology and the social sciences? Or should it make the giant leap, identify itself with black consciousness (despite its many ambiguities) and accept that the future of South Africa – state, Church and people – would finally be decided not by white liberals, but by the corporate expression of black authenticity? It was not an easy decision: it was, and was seen to be, a watershed.

Under the leadership of Beyers Naudé, still a minister of the NGK, the CI chose to commit itself to the struggle for black liberation – a language which itself reflects the new timbre of thought and action. For now the CI was committed to a process of radicalisation which realists predicted (accurately) would destroy it, and which idealists defended as the only way forward that was consistent with both the Gospel of Christ and the realities of the South African situation as analysed by Spro-Cas.

In terms of programme, the CI quickly moved into organising community action in the black townships, while a reconstituted Spro-Cas, now known as Spro-Cas 2, tried, with limited success, to carry the whites and especially the white Churches along the path the CI itself was treading.

The real change, however, lay at a deeper level. The self-understanding of the CI was shifting from that of a white-dominated study and reflection group, to a prophetic community sharing the suffering of the blacks, and learning something in the process about the transforming possibilities of the Cross of Christ. Reflecting on developments within the life and work of the CI over the last four years, Dr Manas Buthelezi had this to say to a rally in Cape Town in October 1974:

> Like a hungry tramp who retrieves crumbs of food from garbage cans, the Christian Institute is seen to be trying to retrieve certain discarded Christian values from the dirt bin of the South African way of life ... The Christian Institute is an outcast in relation to the bulk of powerful white South Africa; ... articulate blacks pitifully doubt its chances of success. Since (Spro-Cas) was tantamount to stepping on the toes of political structures the leadership of both the Christian Institute and Spro-Cas was subjected to one form of suffering or another ... This is what Christians from time immemorial have called the power of the cross. People have often asked what happens after Spro-Cas? My answer is: beyond the message of the theology of Spro-Cas lies the theology of the power of the Cross ... It is the power of the theology of the cross the Christian Institute is now living. Black people can understand this theology because they have always lived it, the theology of power beyond words.[4]

Those last two sentences summarise precisely the nature of confronting the demonic powers in any society. It is living a 'theology of power beyond words', moving out of intellectual debate into a cosmic struggle with the inner essence of evil forces that corrupt and betray whatever individuals and corporate entities they can penetrate. In the case of the Christian Institute, that struggle cost some exile, some imprisonment, most continuous official harassment and private ostracism – and some of its friends' premature death. And yet gloom and despondency had no place in the final word of the CI. Following the eruption of Soweto in June 1976, one of the last issues of *Pro Veritate*, the CI's journal, had this to say:

> Is there no shame when whites must shoot hundreds of school children to maintain their superiority? But Christians who prophesy only doom must realise they are not speaking with a Jesus voice. There is an alternative programme in which the positive contribution of whites is fully demanded, arising from the faith that God is busy with his programme. The strategy of God is at work in our history and it is our task to find and follow his purpose. That is what the Christian faith is about, and the task for which we are sent to make disciples.[5]

A 'theology of power beyond words', for all that it involves facing the cross, does not, at least in the experience of the CI, involve a despairing admission that the demonic powers, either in us as individuals or projected into our structures and institutions, are so strong that they will never be overthrown. So it must have seemed to many, in South Africa and outside it, as they watched the government clamp down on organised dissent in the later months of 1977. There must have been many who felt – and more who now feel – that only violence would overcome the institutionalised violence of the South African state. To hang on to the conviction that the more radical way to end that institutionalised violence is by overcoming the demonic powers that lie at its heart through the Cross and Resurrection of Jesus Christ must have seemed like romantic folly. No doubt it still seems like romantic folly, especially to younger blacks who are weary of Church leaders pleading for moderation and patience.

The question they – and we – have to answer with our lives is then simply put: do we believe that the power of the Cross and

Resurrection have transforming power? or do we believe that we are obliged to settle for the lesser level of political change that violence certainly can effect? Each has to answer that question for him or herself – and those of us who are not in the frontline are well advised to respect the prayerful judgment of those who are. And if, in the end, the choice is the latter, the longer-term need is to proclaim – and live out in as attractive and compelling a way as we are enabled – an affirmative answer to the former. For, in the words of David Jenkins, 'it might be that Christians have to decide how to take sides in the light of the fact that the Christian's basic alignment is always with and for the powerless and that it is the power of powerlessness, when taken up in suffering, absorption, reconciliation and love, which is the one constantly creative and open-ended force at work in the world.'[6]

4 Solidarity

My fourth example is of another 'obvious failure' at the superficial level. It is very different from the other three in that its identity with the official Church is even more ambiguous; its objectives were, in some instances, both more fuzzy and more obviously self-serving and its methods at times perhaps more questionable. I have another difficulty with it which I had better admit. I have no first-hand experience of its environment, no facility in its language, and no personal knowledge of any of the key factors. Yet at times it seems to approach so precisely the kind of confrontation with institutionalised demonic power that I am seeking to illustrate that to leave it out would seem almost a dereliction of duty. Given my inevitable dependence on secondary sources, and the very nature of the political culture, there has to be a degree of provisionality and uncertainty in the following discussion of this example.

I refer, of course, to Solidarity, the network of free self-governing trade unions that flourished in Poland between August 1980 and the imposition of martial law in December 1981. A number of streams came together in the tidal wave of protest that overran Poland in the summer of 1980 – ostensibly a shift in the proportion of meat to be sold in higher-priced shops, but in reality discontent with a low and probably falling standard of living despite official promises of improvement; fury at obvious economic mismanagement of a huge investment programme financed by foreign borrowing; anger at the inadequacy and inequitable distribution of housing, especially in the rapidly growing industrial cities; almost universal contempt for the over-bureaucratisation of even relatively simple procedures and widespread suspicion that senior bureaucrats and especially Party officials were corrupt. This corruption was manifested not only in the way that bribery was required to lubricate the cranky processes of official decision-making, but in the wider sense that 'they' were creaming-off large proportions of available goods and foreign exchange, while ordinary people either went without or queued for several hours for the normal necessities of family life.

Behind and around these issues, however, lay a less tangible one, but one that came to symbolise the essence of the frustration of so many people in Poland: the conviction that the official media of radio, television and newspapers never told the truth, the whole truth. Abolition of the so-called 'propaganda of success' – i.e. the reporting only of those events and achievements which reflected well on the Party and the suppression of anything that suggested failure or incompetence – became one of the earliest and most prized objectives for Solidarity.

August 1980. Here is what Lech Walesa himself has written about it – in a short piece that starts with a quotation from Josef Tischner, the chaplain to Solidarity: 'A lie is a disease of speech.' Walesa goes on:

When in August 1980, a general strike was in progress in Gdansk, party/government newspapers frantically sought deceptive and euphemistic terms to refer to this event. They wrote: 'On the seacoast, spotty interruptions of work have taken place', or, 'An irregularity of supplies has been noticed'... Obviously the issue here was not only about words: the words simply manifested a fear of the truth – truth, suppressed for so long, that exploded with great force. The newspaper prattle was intended to hide the thousands of idle factories and the people in them, full of rebellion and hope... Millions of people were shedding the invisible veneer of a lie and breaking the equally invisible barrier of fear ... today's Solidarity is a communion of the people who do not wish to participate in a lie.[7]

Rebellion and hope: many people were in rebellion against the dreary retailing of half-truth or falsehood, perhaps none more so than those journalists who had maintained some integrity, despite the endless pressure to distort or misrepresent the truth. One of the earliest changes in key personnel after the Gdansk Agreements were signed was that of director of the Press, Radio and TV Department of the Party's Central Committee. The new director, Jozef Klaso, had this to say of the scepticism with which most people treated media reports of political events: 'This distrust is based on experience: we ourselves have taught the people that information is either tendentious or untrue.' In the new atmosphere of relatively free speech Warsaw Radio admitted that 'it used to happen frequently that the head of a department where things were not going too well would, by means of a few telephone calls, make sure that things were reported favourably.[8] Perhaps the most damning indictment, however, came from none other than the new First Secretary, Stanislav Kania, almost immediately after the general strike called by Solidarity on 3 October, 1980. He told the Party's Central Committee that the government had tried to salvage the economy from self-inflicted ruin by increasing prices.

But this was accompanied by hiding or trivialising the true picture of the economic situation and increasing cost of living. Great losses were caused by the so-called propaganda of success, which was conducted with particular insistence by the television service. The biased character of such propaganda did not stand up to commonsense examination. It has to be said honestly at this point that this produced protests among journalists but they were disregarded ... The convention of spreading news only about success left no room for criticism.[9]

It not only left no room for criticism: it bred a cynicism, a distrust and a degree of alienation that workers could now express through Solidarity, especially by using the strike weapon in major industries and the key transport sector[10] to enforce not only access to the media for both Solidarity and the Church, but also a new style of reporting that was so critical that the authorities accused it of becoming a propaganda of defeat. At last, the truth could be told – or at least a higher proportion of it than in any other communist country at any time in history. That achievement is remarkable – for its audacity as well as for its brevity.

What, it may be asked, had the wave of protest that swept through Poland, and especially workers' Poland in 1980 and 1981, to do with the Church? This question is a great deal more complex than may be apparent – and more complex than we can examine in these paragraphs. It is true, but it is not adequate, to say, as so many commentators have done, that the Church, Poland and Solidarity are inseparable. Certainly there is something gripping, perhaps even melodramatic, about the fateful meeting between the Gdansk shipyard workers and deputy prime minister Jagielski in August 1980. The government negotiators sat beneath a statue of Lenin. Lech Walesa and his colleagues sat opposite, under a crucifix. And between them stood a statue of a Polish eagle, the national emblem. Certainly, too, one can point to crucial roles played by priests and Church officials. Rural Solidarity, so bitterly resisted by the government, was led through its most difficult period by a priest. Bogdan Cywinski from the Catholic periodical *Znak* was one of the first nominations to the 'committee of experts', formed on 24 August 1980, to help the Interfactory Strike Committee formulate its negotiating strategy: another was Andrej Wielowiejski of the Catholic Intellectuals' Club.[11] There are many such strands, from the Pope's visit to his native home – and, incidentally, the national shrine the significance of which to Polish nationalist aspirations it is hard to exaggerate – to Cardinal Wyszynski's (initially censored) support of both the Gdansk strike and attempts to register Rural Solidarity.

Yet to leave the story there, as though the Church was Solidarity at prayer, is to overlook three crucial factors. First, the Church had its own agenda throughout the period, and although this overlapped at some crucial points with that of Solidarity, it was not identical to it. For example, from early days the Church played a moderating role, constantly reminding the leadership of Solidarity (itself by no means homogenous, especially after March 1981) of the primacy of averting the disaster that had overtaken Czechoslovakia in not dissimilar circumstances. No wonder the government came to approve of Cardinal Wyszynski so warmly (despite having earlier kept him under house arrest for more than three years). Thus Mieczyslaw Rakowski, editor of the influential journal *Polityka* and a member of the Central Committee (and himself relatively liberal at this stage) endorsed the cardinal's stand with an enthusiasm his subject must have found more than a little ironic:

> The Catholic Church and its leadership, in particular Cardinal Wyszynski, represent a realistic and considered attitude in the present situation. At every turn, they take into consideration Poland's fundamental national interests (i.e. keeping the Russians out). I would like to see a lot of Poles following this path, taking as their example Cardinal Wyszynski, who behaves and acts like a great statesman...[12]

Second, there is some evidence that there was always a gap between the Church and Solidarity – and that this gap grew after the signing of the Gdansk Agreements to the point where key people within Solidarity were openly critical of the Church's role. This criticism stemmed not only from impatience with appeals for moderation precisely when objective analyses were suggesting that the time had come for greater rather than less pressure on the government; but also, and more seriously, from a growing conviction that the Church's own agenda was different *in nature* from that of Solidarity. In his conversations with members of Solidarity in Gdansk, Alain Touraine reports one worker, Powel, as summing up a general feeling thus: 'It sees things from a different point of view to us, and that's why it exerts a stabilising influence.'[13] Touraine concludes: 'It was clear that the movement was quite independent of the Church, especially when the application of the Gdansk Agreement was at stake.'[14]

Third, however, one needs to recognise and honour the fact that, whatever the intricacies of political manoeuvring and personality changes, for many people in Solidarity – and six million had joined in the space of four months – resistance to the government and commitment to 'renewal' had a faith dimension that was expressed most powerfully by the Cross of Christ. The history of resistance to communist rule in central Europe – and especially the events of 1956, 1968 and, most poignantly for most Poles, 1970 – pointed ineluctably to the cross as historical fact. To Poles, however, the experience of the cross in history goes back much further in time, so that as a Solidarity militant in Warsaw put it – and Touraine attests that he was 'summarising everyone's feelings': 'The cross symbolises a set of spiritual values which define us as a nation. We have always wanted to be the subjects, the creators of our national life and not just a labouring mass. The feeling of being treated like objects was crucial in bringing about what is happening now, and it was the church which made us conscious of that.' It is this meld of community (and, possibly, class) assertion, national consciousness and spiritual values that was the common bond between Solidarity and the Church. Programatically, that implied particular unanimity on the abolition of the propaganda of success; the establishment of rights of association; rejection of violence, intimidation and arbitrary arrest; and the choice of a strategy of resistance that would not jeopardise Polish integrity. This last point, however, nearly tore Solidarity apart, leading to some of the more militant members charging that Walesa was far too influenced by the Church and its demands for moderation, patience and even accommodation.

In what ways, then, does Solidarity illustrate the notion of a Christian centre of resistance? It is clearly a very different animal to the Witness for Peace, the peace movement and the Christian Institute. More overtly secular, more ambivalent in its attitude to the institutional Church, more fragmented locationally and ideologically, it wielded a power that none of the other three could ever aspire to. While it is arguable that in the end it was Solidarity's misuse of that very power that made the fall of Kania and the declaration of martial law inevitable, for much of 1980 and 1981 the threat of strike action by Solidarity was enough to achieve advances that hitherto had seemed utopian dreams – the sacking of 1200 corrupt Party officials; the suspension of censorship; the establishment of free trade unions, even of unions of independent private farmers; greater equity in the distribution of housing; a reassessment (albeit short-lived) of the role of the Party in a communist state; even 'free' elections to the Party Congress and the subsequent loss of position of many of the Party's power-brokers. These are spectacular advances by any standards – and almost breathtaking by contemporary standards of Eastern Europe. That they did not last has everything to do with Poland's exposed geo-political position, especially in the military geography of the Warsaw Pact. It has much less to do with the surrender of ideals and values that have not even now been wholly extinguished. Walesa can still speak of rebellion and hope.

As a postscript it is worth drawing attention once again to the moderating role the Church played, almost from the beginning of Solidarity. I want to emphasise that to dispel the impression that might otherwise be created that I see the role of the Church as necessarily in the van of the resistance movement. There is one sense, a spiritual one, in which that must be true. More generally, however, the institutional Church's role may be to protect, warn, advise and restrain a more secularly based movement which has adopted the same values and confronts the same powers as the Church herself.

It is to that issue that we must now turn.

5 Centres of Resistance and Institutional Church

Three of the four examples of confronting the powers I have described are drawn from the First and Second worlds. This is deliberate, as I have argued that the responsibility of the Church in the richer countries is to confront the embodiment of the corrupt powers in their own societies, especially as those powers impact upon the poor at home and abroad. This is not to deny, of course, that it is also the calling of Christians in poorer countries to undertake the same hazardous business. In discussing conscientisation and empowerment of basic communities, I suggested that the pedagogy of the oppressed and the living out of a gospel of liberation are analytically and experientially so closely allied that they become inseparable. The difference between what I have been describing as 'confronting the powers' and Freire's methodology is essentially that I have laid emphasis on the spiritual realities of evil *behind* the structures of injustice, and have accordingly suggested that it is at that level that the powers have to be confronted.

The emphasis I have placed on this spiritual struggle leaves two final questions to be asked. They have hovered in the background of the four case studies I have presented but now need to be faced squarely. First, is this process of confronting the powers for the sake of their transformation the task of the whole Church or for small communities within it? And if the latter, what is the relationship between such small communities and the institutional Church?

This is a complex and difficult field, a subject for a book in itself. For ultimately it is a question about the conversion of the Church. Can the institutional Church ever face, head-on, the political and spiritual corruption of international terrorism in Central America, or institutionalised violence in South Africa? Can she live out a source of security that makes cruise, Pershing and SDI look ridiculous? Can she live a standard of truth that calls to judgment a propaganda of success? Can she, in a word, risk her institutional life for the sake of the Kingdom of her founder?

The evidence we have reviewed – or at least touched on – does not make for easy optimism. The split within the Roman Catholic Church throughout Central (and, for that matter, Latin) America, between, for a Nicaraguan example Cardinal Obando y Bravo and Ernesto Cardenal, hardly encourages us to expect that the whole Church will join in a costly witness against American support for the Contras. The whole history of the Christian Institute in South Africa is, amongst other things, a history of a struggle with and within the institutional Churches (and not only the NHK and the NGK). Many aspects of the Church's life in 1970 were deeply racist and even today, as violence in the townships reaches proportions that make earlier eruptions look like pimples, there are many in the mainline Churches, both clergy and laity, who want to find a *modus vivendi* with the state – which explains, for example, why they found the Kairos document so offensive. We see the same deep divisions with respect to nuclear disarmament – in nearly every institution of Church government in all mainline Churches in the UK, the US and continental Europe. The Roman Catholic Church may have been more or less solidly behind Solidarity, but it is legitimate to ask whether the elevation of Father Tischner did not represent a desire to accommodate rather than continue to confront.

This plurality of political viewpoint is not *necessarily* a sign of weakness or even of a refusal to take adequate account of the demonic powers: though it has to be said that often it is exactly that. I am sometimes told that I expect too much of the institutional Church; that, in the words of an American feminist theologian, I am 'Over-invested in the perfectability of a corrupt, human institution'. Certainly, it is easy to forget of what flawed material the primitive Church was constituted: as a student once put it, having struggled through the Greek text of Matthew 16:18 in which Peter is declared to be the rock on which the Church will be founded: 'Hell's teeth! Some rock.' The Church is an open, undemanding catch-all of saints and sinners; and of saints who know they are sinners; and of sinners who aspire to be saints; and, too, of a great mid-tide wash of humanity that know not what they are but wish, at some level of their inner selves, that they were something other than they find themselves to be. It is the glory as well as the shame of the Church that she is so utterly human that she sometimes, perhaps nearly always, occludes the divine. And yet, for all her frailty and her cruelty, she is loved and accepted – and forgiven and called forward.

If the Church is like each of us individually, a cross of adder and angel yet on a pilgrimage from the essence of the former to the essence of the latter, it is illusory to expect from the whole Church as institution the kind of confrontation of the powers that I have been describing. But nor, emphatically, is that confrontation a matter for the élite, the spiritual shock-troops, the highly trained specialists. It is for those who are called to it, who hear that call, who know that their journeys – both outward and inward – have reached that point where obedience demands they resist with all the force at their command the incorporated evil that impoverishes the poor and wounds the vulnerable. My own suspicion is that that call comes surprisingly early in the journey – and that most of us most of the time do our best to drown it out or to ignore it.

Let us assume that there are a number of centres of resistance that form around specific issues – as the Christian Institute formed round the issue of apartheid as a state ideology, or

Solidarity around the issue of truth in the media. The question then is how are we to see their relationship to the institutional Church? I suggest there are a number of possibilities.

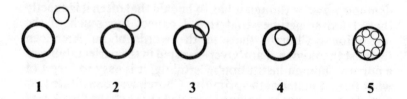

1   2   3   4   5

If, in each of the diagrams above, the smaller circle represents the centre of resistance and the larger the institutional Church, then we can read diagrams 1 to 5 as a kind of progression. In diag. 1, the centre of resistance is quite outside the Church, unconnected to it in any way. This is the model that many ecclesiastical authorities in Latin America and Asia fear of the conscientised communities of peasants, the basic communities. An attempt may be made to link them as in 1a:

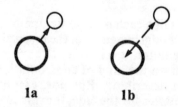

1a   1b

where, for example, a priest is attached to a basic community or where members of a centre of resistance are given roles or status within the institutional Church. At some time in the history of Solidarity, especially in Gdansk, it is clear that this was the nature of the relationship. There are parallels, too, with some elements of the peace movement in both the UK and the US. Naturally the difficulty with this relationship is that it very easily becomes so strained that the link breaks (1b). The force of the break may then project the two entities even further apart – almost certainly to the diminishment of both.

Diagrams 2–4 show various stages, from 2 where the centre of resistance has minimal contact with the institutional Church (CND in the UK) to 4 where the centre of resistance is wholly within the Church, though still on the edge. (Arguably this was the position, at least at some stages of their history, of both the Christian Institute, perhaps in its early years, and the Witness for Peace.)

Diagram 5 represents an extension of Diagram 4, where the whole (or nearly the whole) of the 'space' of the institutional Church is taken up by centres of resistance, each supporting and being supported by the other.

There is danger in letting these simple diagrams run away with the argument, so that, for example, we become over-interested in the centre of the circle representing the Church or the nature of the common arc in Diagram 3. I think it important, however, properly to honour the necessity of the institutional Church – as bearer of the tradition, as spiritual womb of the centres of resistance, as the continuo that sustains more exciting or more lyrical passages in the opera of God's redeeming work. It is thus not part of my argument to belittle or condemn the role of the institutional Church – as institutional Church. It is not – and is unlikely to become – a cluster of centres of resistance, as in model 5. If it can spawn, nourish and leave space for such centres – models 2 to 4 – then it is playing a legitimate part in confronting the powers with the redeeming possibility of Christ. If, however, it does the reverse of those things – kills, starves, constricts – then the Church itself becomes a scandal.

That is, however, to polarise the issue unrealistically. As the examples I have quoted suggest, the institutional Church *both* nourishes *and* starves, *both* spawns *and* kills. That is the nature of her being, the outcome of her role in the history of redemption. She is an interim creature, a first fruit, and therefore *both* adder *and* angel. She eats her young with insouciance; but she protects them with ferocity and self-sacrifice. In this as in all things, she lives by grace; and she, just as we and our secular institutions, stands constantly in need of all the grace she may be given. If she forgets that too often and too easily, so that she again becomes domineering or cruel or a counter-sign of resurrection life, she – and we – need to remember that God's purposes may be worked out in other fora, through other agendas. God has never allowed Himself to be restricted to one humanly fallible, often wayward or silly people. We need not be surprised, therefore, if sometimes we detect the echo of Jeremiah's words on the people of Israel:

Call them spurious silver;
for the Lord has spurned them. (Jer. 6:30)

Epilogue

It may seem that we have come a long way from where we started – with a telephone call to the headquarters of a Church development agency at the very beginning of the Ethiopian crisis. In one sense that is true, for confronting the Powers of our systems, institutions and structures involves a very different area of discourse and operating style from raising money for the relief of famine. In another sense, however, we are back where we started, facing the reality of human suffering and being drawn to ask how we may properly respond to that reality.

In these final paragraphs it is not my purpose to overdraw that contrast. I do not, for example, wish to deny the importance of emergency relief or, for that matter, project assistance. There are – and no doubt always will be – organisations, both secular and Church-related, for which that represents an appropriate area of work. What can never be right, however, is for the work of those organisations to *define* an adequate Christian response to the processes of impoverishment, oppression and dehumanisation that we have unearthed in the course of this book. When once the parameters of Christian response are set purely in terms of the organisations' own objectives – either by their conscious effort (for example, to protect their image and/or fundraising capacity) or by our corporate failure to specify a wider agenda – they become demonic. And we connive with that demon.

For to continue to act as though the poverty of nearly a billion people can be eliminated by aided projects is to fail to take seriously both the nature of the problem and the nature of the world. It does not take seriously the nature of the problem because it ignores the structures within which mass poverty is set – and by which it is perpetuated. It does not take seriously the nature of the world because it ignores the Powers that, as it were, hold the world in thrall. More damagingly than either, it consequently ignores the *scale* of the work of Christ in Cross, Resurrection and Pentecost. In this it is, to all intents and purposes, indistinguishable from an enlightened liberal humanism.

The agenda I have implied in the last three chapters is radically different. It is, however, an agenda that is already being explored – by the base communities in Latin America (and in Italy and France); by a whole rash of new communities in the rich North, from the Sojourners in the United States, to tiny little cells of people who are discovering the inter-penetration of prayer and praxis in their own situation. This is the agenda I have called alternative consciousness – a level of understanding, acting, believing and hoping that rejects the reductionism of liberal humanism, and engages with the world at the level from which permanent change must come.

I have suggested that alternative consciousness finds expression in the creation and sustenance of centres of resistance – resistance, that is, to the Powers that threaten destruction to the human possibilities with which we are all – individually and corporately – presented. We have to face the fact, however, that it is not easy to find model centres of resistance to the Powers that dominate the structures that we have identified as central in this volume – international trade, the international monetary system, technology, Western consumerism, the net. We did find two models that confront the Powers of militarism and two that confront totalitarianism. And that raises a final sombre point.

Each of the models, even the Witness for Peace, springs from a threat to those who constitute the centre of resistance. That is more clearly true in the case of the peace movements and Solidarity than of the other two, but the fear of a racial holocaust in the case of the Christian Institute and of a re-run of the Vietnam disaster in the case of the Witness for Peace cannot easily be discounted. To say that is to impugn neither the altruism nor the courageous sincerity of those associated with either of these enterprises. It is, however, to acknowledge that we Christians may have to travel a lot further on the inward journey before we shall finally have died sufficiently to self to become the stuff out of which centres of resistance, genuinely in solidarity with the poor of the world, may be constructed.

Yet that is precisely what we should expect. According to two evangelists, Jesus's last formal teaching of the disciples was about humility and service, the defeat of the clamant ego. Little changes...

Is that, then, where we have to start? Is the journey to alternative consciousness a journey, first, to do battle with that power of self-will that is the most fundamental form of idolatry – at both individual and institutional levels? I believe so, but I believe, too, that that is only the start of the journey – or, to change the metaphor slightly, that that is one road down which we are all called. And the more we are struck by global injustice or even by the bare facts of global poverty, the more certainly, if more paradoxically, are we obliged to tread that road.

It follows then that when I am asked for an instant action guide at the end of a book like this, I have to start at that point. For I do not believe that we can separate, either analytically or programmatically (in the way most of the Church development agencies have mistakenly tried to do), the call to individual holiness from the call to global justice. That the two are not identical or that the former is only one condition of the latter is, I hope, in no further need of elaboration at this stage. Let me, however, repeat: if we are to take global injustice seriously, we have to start by dealing with the roots of that injustice in each one of us. To fail to do that with ultimate seriousness is to flirt with the role of the hypocrite.

How we do that is simply not open to instant solution. People come to this from different backgrounds, with different experiences, expectations, fears, hopes and bruises. The creative way for one will be deathly for another. In the first part of Chapter 10 I tried to indicate what seem to be the constituent elements for most people: certainly what has proven central for me personally. It would, however, be as arrogant as it would be misleading to suggest that the elements I describe there are normative for everyone. Each has to find his or her way. That takes time, effort, imagination, discipline and perseverance. It is work.

And it brings pain. As we confront the powers that dominate us and our structures, and as we explore how we are incorporated in the cosmic drama, both in its conflict and, 'in Christ', its final outcome, we are likely to discover that we share in the wounds of the universe – and that we contribute our wounds to the universe. It is in that discovery of our woundedness that we both share in and are healed by the Cross of Christ – and are thereby gradually freed from the grip of the Powers that dominate us.

To those who want a simple formula, a straight answer to the seemingly straight question: 'What do I do now?' I can only reply 'Try it'. There *are* no simple formulae – and those who claim to dispense them are either naive or wicked. There are, however, friends, companions, communities of fellow pilgrims on the way. Some people find a single 'soul friend', in Ken Leeche's titular phrase, an important guide; others prefer to mingle with the crowd, and give and take whatever opportunity affords. Either way, we are neither called nor expected to withstand the rigours of the journey all alone.

So much for the inward journey. The outward journey is likely to contain a number of elements, but the blend of those elements will again be very largely a matter of personal 'fit' or fittingness. The inward journey will help clarify that fit, as will trial and error. The main elements are likely to be:

(i) the work of the mind: learning the facts; doing the analysis; testing the truth; sorting truth from falsehood from oversimplification from exaggeration from special plea.

(ii) the work of the heart: mobilising imagination, empathy and emotional solidarity with the vulnerable, the despised and the marginal wherever they may be; but also learning to see even the rich and powerful in all their trappedness, especially their institutional and cosmic trappedness.

(iii) the work of the hands: active engagement in that part of 'the problem' which most comes alive in both the inner journey and in the work of mind and heart above. This engagement will be in response to a heart-deep showing of the love of Christ, rather than to a sense of guilt or shame or anger.

(iv) the work of the feet: to put us in contact with fellow pilgrims. Whether or not we choose to make the inward journey nearly alone, the outward journey will involve us in communion with others – in at least three senses of that word.

We shall need to communicate with them (learn from them, share with them). We shall need to hold things in common with them – ideals, hopes, maybe possessions. We shall need to express and draw upon our common allegiance to the Christ who vanquishes the powers we learn to identify and confront.

Again we must be careful not to be too neat. For those four 'works' interact with each other dialectically. Sharing with others (especially the marginal) en-ables, en-courages the work of the heart; and as that begins to come alive so it will redirect the work of the hands – and incidentally inspire the inward journey. And as that progresses, so the powers – individual, institutional and cosmic – are revealed and faced.

That is all they are, however. They are not thereby transformed and transcended. We shall burn out or break down if we imagine that it is within our competence to do what Christ alone can do – and has done. All we can do is ally ourselves with His work and then receive it as a gift.

And it is on that note that it is well to finish. I am aware that much of this book is painted in sombre colours. Conflict, pain, suffering, persecution, rejection, poverty, failure, weakness – these have been the recurrent motifs, as we have moved in from the simplistic solutions of the development agencies and their ecclesiastical counterparts to a more realistic assessment of the nature of the problem. I make no apology for that. I believe it to be the truth – the truth of the cosmos and the truth of Christ. But it is only part of the truth.

The rest of the truth – that 'God so loved the world...' – transforms the sombre account I have given and, without denying the reality of the pain of the journey to which we are called, offers us a Companion whose joy is infectious, whose laughter is never long silent and who knows better how to dance than to hobble – despite the holes in His feet. It is good to dance with Him.

Notes

Chapter 2

1. There is an extensive literature on and a vigorous debate about the work of the missions and its effect on colonised peoples. See, for example, Stephen Neill: *A history of Christian missions*, Penguin, Harmondsworth, 1977.
2. C. Ehrlich, *The Uganda Company, The First Fifty Years*, Kampala, 1953.
3. Polly Hill, *Migrant Cocoa Farmers of Southern Ghana*, CUP, Cambridge, 1963. p. 165.
4. On one estimate, probably on the low side, the resources mobilised by the voluntary sector in the US for development tripled from $200m to $600m 1960–68. This excludes co-funding from public sources. J.E. Sommer: *Beyond charity: U.S. voluntary aid for a changing Third World*, ODC, Washington, 1977. I know of no strictly comparable figures for the UK but there is no doubt that the major development charities grew rapidly in the 1960s.
5. Julius Nyerere, *Freedom and Unity; Uhuru no Umoja. A selection from writings and speeches 1952–1965*, OUP, Dar-es-Salaam, 1967, pp. 37, 43.
6. See Vincent J. Donovan, *Christianity Rediscovered. An Epistle from the Masai*, SCM, London, 1978.
7. Membership of the Tanganyika African National Union was considered a disqualification for employment on a mission at any level. See Nyerere op. cit., p. 100.
8. P.H. Gruber (ed.) *Fetters of Injustice. Report of an ecumenical consultation on ecumenical assistance to development projects*, WCC, Geneva, 1970, pp. 24–5.

Chapter 3

1. That this is a thing of the past is an illusion that is betrayed by the evidence. See, for example, Catherine Price, *British Aid to Tanzania*, Independent Group on British Aid, London, 1986. American aid has been – and continues to be – heavily influenced by political considerations. See T. Hayter with Catherine Watson, *Aid, Rhetoric and Reality*, Pluto, London, 1985.
2. Noel Drogat, S.J., *Le Chrétien et L'aide aux pays sous développés: documents et données statistiques*, Centurion, Paris, 1962.

3. Paul Abrecht, 'Issues for Christians', in Denys Munby (ed.) *Economic Growth in World Perspective*, Associated, New York, SCM, London, 1966, p. 375.
4. Gunnar Myrdal, *Asian Drama*, Pantheon, New York, 1968.
5. S.A. Aluko, 'The dynamics of economic growth in the developing countries', in Munby, sup. cit.

Chapter 4

1. There was, for example, a call for a 'moratorium' on church development aid in Africa from the All Africa Council of Churches in 1968. The pressures that led to that demand were contained by the donor agencies, but it emerged, in less formal terms, from time to time. As recently as 1985, a conference of younger Church development workers in Africa, again convened by the AACC, discussed a moratorium and decided not to recommend it formally only because, in the view of the participants, African Church leaders would not, in the end, support it.
2. Michael Lipton, *Why poor people stay poor: a study of urban bias in world development*, Temple Smith, London, 1977.
3. Some, of course, were better equipped in this respect than others. The leading British Church agency employed no one with a relevant social science degree until the late 1970s. The American and German agencies tended to employ better trained staff, but seldom people who could subject their technical qualifications to theological critique. The more separated from the mainline life of the Churches the donor agencies became, the more needed was such a critique – and the less likely was it that it would be supplied from outside the agency.

Chapter 5

1. See Evan Luard, *The Management of the World Economy*, Macmillan, London, 1983, pp. 78ff.
2. Gruber, op. cit., pp. 124-5.
3. See Magnus Blomstrom and Bjorn Hettne, *Development Theory in Transition*, Zed Press, London, 1984, pp. 38-45.
4. R. Prebisch, *Towards a dynamic development policy for Latin America*, UN, New York, 1963; and H. Singer, 'The distribution of gains between investing and borrowing countries', *American Economic Review, Papers and Proceedings*, Vol. II, no. 2, May 1950.
5. Prebisch and Singer did not have it all their own way. See, for example, June Flanders, 'Prebisch on protectionism: an evaluation,' *Economic Journal* Vol. LXXIV no. 294 June 1964. Nor is their view even now universally acclaimed. See C.B. Edwards, *The fragmented world: competing perspectives on trade, money and crises*, Methuen, London, 1985.

6. See, for example R. Clignet and P. Foster, *The Fortunate Few – a study of secondary schools and students in the Ivory Coast*, Evanston, Ill., 1966.
7. Oscar Gish, *Planning the Health Sector: The Tanzanian experience*, Croom Helm, London, 1975. The astonishing thing is that ten years after Gish's book appeared – and nearly twenty years after the basic point had been well understood – the proportion of the health budget of Tanzania spent on primary health care remained at the same low level.
8. R.E. Koplin, *Education and national integration in Ghana and Kenya*, Ph.D. dissertation, Oregon, 1968. The figures would, of course, be much more adverse if one compared the chances of an upper class *boy* with those of a poor *girl*, perhaps by a factor of three.
9. A. Giddens has written much on these themes. See his *Studies in social and political theory*, Hutchinson, London, 1977.
10. Cosmas Desmond, *Christians or Capitalists? Christianity and Politics in South Africa*, Bowerdean, London, 1978.
11. Brian Griffiths, *The moral basis of the market economy*, CPC, London, 1985.
12. Digby Anderson (ed.), *The Kindness that kills*, SPCK, London, 1985.
13. *North-South: A programme for survival. The Report of the Independent Commission on International Development Issues under the chairmanship of Willy Brandt*, Pen, London, 1980.
14. See, for example, C. Price, sup. cit.

Chapter 6

1. The one counter example of which I have had personal experience was the Irish Catholic agency Trocaire which invited representatives of the 'travelling people' to a major conference. When these representatives made a passionate and well-argued case for help in righting what they experience as injustice, the organisers of the conference ruled them out of order and ensured their presentation was never discussed.
2. T. Scarlett Epstein and R.A. Watts (eds.), *The endless day: some case material on Asian rural women*, Pergamon, Oxford, 1981, and Barbara Rogers, *The domestication of women: discrimination in developing societies*, Kegan Page, London, 1980.
3. Figures from *World Development Report 1983*, World Bank, Washington. China and India are excluded from the poorest countries covered by this statistic.
4. *The Net: Power Structure in Ten Villages*, Bangladesh Rural Advancement Committee, Dacca, Bangladesh, February 1980, mimeo.
5. Oscar Lewis, *The Children of Sanchez*, Random House, N.Y., 1961. *La Vida*, Random House, New York, 1966.
6. The effects of the Green Revolution on the structure of land holding is a deeply debated issue and regional variations are clearly very important. For a recent summary of the evidence, see T. Bailey-Smith and Sudhir

Wanmali (eds.), *Understanding Green Revolutions – agrarian change and development planning in South Asia*. Cambridge University Press, Cambridge, 1984.
7. See Ray Bromley (ed.), *Planning for small enterprises in Third World cities*, Pergamon, Oxford.
8. Walter Wink, *Naming the Powers. The Language of Power in the New Testament*: Vol I., *The Powers*, Fortress, Philadelphia, 1984.

Chapter 7

1. Paulo Freire, *Pedagogy of the oppressed*, Penguin, Harmondsworth, 1972.
2. A good summary with some interesting examples is Peadar Kirby, *Lessons in Liberation*, Dominican, Dublin, 1981.
3. For an account of such adaptation in a totally different cultural setting, see Donal Dorr, *Spirituality and Justice*, Gill & Macmillan/Orbis, Dublin/New York, 1984, pp. 150–8.
4. Ernesto Cardenal, *Love in Practice: the Gospel in Solentiname*, Search, London, 1977.
5. See Joseph Collins with Frances Moore Lappé and Nick Allen: *What difference could a revolution make? Food and Farming in the new Nicaragua*, 2nd revised edition, Institute for Food and Development Policy, San Francisco, 1985.
6. See, for instance, J.M. Bonino, *Doing theology in a revolutionary situation*, Philadelphia, 1976.

Chapter 8

1. Andre Gunder Frank, *Latin America: Underdevelopment or Revolution? Essays on the development of underdevelopment*, Monthly Review Press, New York and London, 1969, p. 59.
2. Colin Leys, *Underdevelopment in Kenya. The Political Economy of Neo-Colonialism 1964–1971*, London, 1975. The first chapter has a useful survey of early dependency theory.
3. There is, however, a great deal of debate between Marxists and neo-Marxists about this. See Aidan Foster-Carter: 'From Rostow to Gunder Frank: "Conflicting paradigms in the analysis of underdevelopment"', *World Development* Vol. 4, no. 3, 1976.
4. I. Oxaal *et al., Beyond the Sociology of Development*, Routledge Kegan Paul, London, 1975. See too Blomstrom and Hette op. cit. pp. 179–182.

Chapter 9

1. Walter Wink, *Naming the Powers. The Language of Power in the New*

    Testament, Vol. 1., *The Powers,* Fortress, Philadelphia, 1984, pp. 7–9.

2. This paragraph and the next are taken largely from my 1983 CMS Annual Sermon, *Power, Salvation and Suffering,* Church Missionary Society, 1983.

3. M. Hengel, *Christ and Power,* Christian Journals/Marshall Pickering, Belfast/London, 1977, p. 81.

4. Ernest Fuchs, *Zur Frage nach dem historischen Jesus,* Mohr. Tubingen, 1960. Quoted in Hengel, op. cit., p. 21.

5. David Jenkins, 'The Power of the Powerless', in *In Search of a Theology of Development,* Sodepax/WCC, Geneva, 1970, pp. 51–3.
    Jurgen Moltmann, *The Power of the Powerless,* SCM, London, 1983.

6. James Crampsey, Jesus and Power, *The Way.* Vol. 26, No. 3., July 1986, p. 186.

7. Op. cit., p. 105.

8. Op. cit. p. 111.

9. Leonardo Boff, *St. Francis. A Model for Human Liberation,* SCM, London, 1985.

10. See, for example, Christopher Bryant, *The Power Within: The Search for God in Depth,* DLT, London, 1978.

11. Quoted by Ted Kennedy in: 'Called to be Powerless?', *The Way,* Vol. 26., No. 3., July, 1986, p. 197.

12. William Stringfellow, *An Ethic for Christians and Other Aliens in a Strange Land,* Word Inc., Texas, 1973, pp. 93–4.

13. *Capital I,* Penguin, Harmondsworth, 1976, p. 799. For a more scholarly treatment of Marx on alienation, on which I have drawn in these paragraphs, see N. Lash, *A Matter of Hope,* Darton, Longman, Todd, London, 1983, pp. 173ff.

Chapter 10

1. See, for example, Kim Yong-Bock: 'Korean Christianity as a Messianic Movement of the People', in Commission on theological concerns of the Christian Conference of Asia (eds.) *Minjung Theology: People as the subjects of history,* Zed Press, London and Orbis, Maryknoll, New York, 1983, pp. 80–119.

2. Reprinted as *Challenge to the Church: A theological comment on the Political Crisis in South Africa,* CIIR/RCC, London, 1985.

3. See, for example, Martin Israel, *Summons to Life. The search for identity through the spiritual,* Hodder & Stoughton, London, 1974, pp. 51–7.

4. Martin Marty, *The Cry of Absence,* Harper & Row, San Francisco, 1983, p. 5.

5. See Philip L. Wicken, 'Theological Reorientation in Chinese Protestantism, 1949–84, in *Ching Feng. Quarterly Notes on Christianity and Chinese Religion and Culture,* V & XXVIII No. 1, March 1985.

6. Thomas Merton, *The Seven Storey Mountain*, Harcourt, Brace, New York, 1948, p. 232.
7. Thomas Cullinan OSB: *The Church as an agent of social change – from the edge* (mimeo), Ince Benet, 1985.
8. The average figure for IDA eligible countries in Sub-Saharan Africa 1986–90 is projected to be twenty-eight per cent. By 1990 it will be thirty-four per cent. World Bank: *Financing Adjustment with Growth in Sub Saharan Africa, 1986–90,* Washington DC, 1986, p. 56. Tab. A.4.
9. C.S. Song, *Third Eye Theology,* Lutterworth, London, 1983.

Chapter 11

1. SIPRI *Arms Trade in the Third World,* Harmondsworth, Penguin, 1975. W. Brandt, *World Disarmament and world hunger*, Harmondsworth, Penguin, 1986.
2. From the Message to the People of South Africa, published in September, 1968. Quoted in John W. de Gruchy: 'A short history of the Christian Institute', in Charles Villa-Vicencio and John W. de Gruchy (eds.) *Resistance and Hope. South African essays in honour of Beyers Naudé*, David Philip, Cape Town/William Eerdmans, Grand Rapids, 1985.
3. ibid, p. 21.
4. ibid, p. 23.
5. ibid, p. 26.
6. Jenkins, sup. cit.
7. Lech Walesa, Afterword: in Jozef Tischner, *The Spirit of Solidarity*, Harper & Row, San Francisco, 1984, p. 105.
8. Kevin Ruane, *The Polish Challenge,* BBC, London, 1982, pp. 79, 80.
9. ibid, p. 56.
10. The transport sector was particularly sensitive since the Russians depended on it for access to East Germany and their defence installations there.
11. Alain Touraine, *Solidarity. The Analysis of a Social Movement: Poland 1980–81*, CUP, Cambridge, 1983, pp. 68ff.
12. Ruane, sup. cit., p. 69.
13. Touraine, sup. cit., p. 147.
14. ibid.
15. ibid, p. 48.

INDEX